BY THE SAME AUTHOR

ATTITUDES OF AMAZING ACHIEVERS
WISDOM OF WEALTHY ACHIEVERS
WISDOM – THE FORGOTTEN FACTOR OF SUCCESS

Copyright © 2004 Philip Leonard Baker

The author asserts the moral right
to be identified as the author of this work

A Lion Book
an imprint of
Lion Hudson plc
Mayfield House, 256 Banbury Road
Oxford OX2 7DH, England
www.lionhudson.com
ISBN-13: 978-0-7459-5212-3
ISBN-10: 0-7459-5212-7

First edition 2004
10 9 8 7 6 5 4 3 2 1 0

Design by The Globe Advertising and Design

A catalogue record for this book is available
from the British Library

Typeset in 10/15 New Baskerville

Printed and bound in Great Britain
by Cox and Wyman Ltd.

SECRETS OF SUPER ACHIEVERS

PHILIP BAKER

LION

To the four ladies of my life.

Heather, Jazmin, Temily and Isabel.

CONTENTS

ACKNOWLEDGMENTS i

FOREWORD WHY EQUALITY IS NOT FOR US iii

CHAPTER 1 THE QUEST FOR CHARACTER 1
Inward and Onward

CHAPTER 2 JUST A PUPPET ON A STRING 15
Responsibility

CHAPTER 3 DAZE OF OUR LIVES 25
Overriding Goal or Passion

CHAPTER 4 YOU HAVE TO JUMP IN THE PUDDLES 39
Optimism

CHAPTER 5 FATAL DISTRACTION 53
Focus

CHAPTER 6 IT'S NOT CHECK OUT TIME YET 63
Endurance

CHAPTER 7 IN PRAISE OF TALL POPPIES 81
Abundance Mentality

CHAPTER 8 MY BRAIN HURTS 93
Constant Learning

CHAPTER 9 LIFESTYLES OF THE RICH AND MISERABLE 107
Contentment

CHAPTER 10 FLYING WITH THE DUCKS 119
People Believers

CHAPTER 11	KEEPING OUT OF THE DITCHES	129
	Balance	
CHAPTER 12	FIRST YOU HAVE TO GET OUT OF BED	139
	Discipline	
CHAPTER 13	I'M BIGGER ON THE INSIDE	151
	Self-Growth	
CHAPTER 14	THE UPSIDE OF DOWN	159
	Humility	
CHAPTER 15	FORTUNE FAVOURS THE BRAVE	173
	Courage	
EPILOGUE	FURTHER ON, FURTHER IN	183
AUTHOR		188
BIBLIOGRAPHY		189

ACKNOWLEDGMENTS

I would like to thank:

My wife, Heather, for her love and the incentive plan.

Penny Webb for her encouragement and confidence in me. It was her hard work that converted the ideas of this book into that which you hold in your hand.

Wes Beavis, who kept telling me to write a book and was most helpful in scrutinizing the text, pre-publication.

The many friends, students and co-workers who read and reread the early drafts of this book – Mark Webb, Mark Pomery, Christine Reeves, Bree Elliott, Jillian MacLachlan, Moira McLean, Pat Mesiti, Graham Irvine, Pam Howie and Rosemary Crooks.

All those who call Riverview Church their home. The great privilege of leading a church, and the thinking and speaking such a position entails, gave me the place and the reason to communicate things that really matter.

FOREWORD
WHY EQUALITY IS NOT FOR US

'Great men are little men
expanded; great lives are
ordinary lives intensified.'

Wilfred A. Peterson

I believe that every human being has been created with greatness in mind. Within us all is a deep well of incredible potential. Bob Richards, the Olympic pole-vaulter, put it this way: '*There is genius in every person.*' Zig Ziglar's favourite expression runs along similar lines: '*People are designed for accomplishment, engineered for success, and endowed with the seeds of greatness.*' While I believe these sentiments with all my heart, I realize that not all reach their potential. Indeed, very few could die totally satisfied with the fact that they did everything, and were everything they could have been.

I have spent most of my life thinking and speaking along these lines. How can I be all that I could be? How can I help others realize their potential? A tragedy of life is that many of us settle for just getting by, rather than success. We have developed a maintenance mentality that minimizes the pain in life but does not strive for the mastery. We look up to those who excel and call them lucky or blessed. We want to be like them and often try to imitate their behaviour and learn from their life.

It is easy, however, with such an undertaking, to focus on the wrong thing, to try to copy the actions, skills and practices of the successful, rather than getting to the heart, the inner working of such a life.

Most of us want to be who we were designed to be and to live a life of excellence. Over the process of time we learn that what is within us is the principal thing. We begin to draw water from the reservoirs of our soul and come to the realization that our future is flexible. We can set our own level in life. This understanding alone causes us to raise our expectations, and as a result, rise and live an abundant life.

Unfortunately others respond in a more negative way to the successful individual. Their hearts are filled with envy, secretly delighting in the failure of others and critical of any that are achieving beyond the norm. Such smallness of spirit is the seed-bed for both the tall poppy syndrome and the town gossip. George Gilder, in examining this human phenomenon and its impact upon the economics of community and nations, gives an illustration from the work of Edward Banfield, *The Moral Basis of a Backward Society.*

> *'In a small town in Italy that he studied, in an effort to understand the sources of poverty, every businessman was assumed to be cheating his employees, every priest to be filching from the plate, every politician and policeman to be on the take. A teacher justified his laziness by confiding that the only use of education was to better exploit the poor. Any signs of prosperity were taken as evidence of peculation or crime. Needless to say, in such a town few such signs appeared.'*[1]

Such people's basic philosophy is that, despite effort and initiative, we are all meant to be the same and have the

same in life. Anything else is either evidence of
wrongdoing or simply just unfair.

Personally, I believe that life is not and cannot be this
way. Things such as wisdom, hard work and the willingness
to go the extra mile do actually make a difference. Life
is not a zero sum game. Egalitarianism, that thinks nothing
of punishing achievement and rewarding inactivity and
laziness, must be quashed from our consciousness if we
are to rise to new levels in life.

Yes, we have incredible potential but we will only achieve
in life when we begin to stretch ourselves and realize that
a life of abundance will not just happen because we are
good people. We need to do things, believe things and
think in new ways. This book is all about becoming a Super
Achiever in life. It is written to the person who desires to
plumb the depths of his or her own being and grow. To
the person not satisfied to simply be. To those who want
to move beyond mediocrity and push themselves to excel.

REFERENCES

[1] George Gilder, *Wealth and Poverty*, ICS, 1993, p. 110.

CHAPTER 1
THE QUEST FOR CHARACTER
Inward and Onward

'The new frontier of the '90s is an inner one.'

Peggy Noonan, President George Bush Snr's Speech Writer.

The concept of character is often quoted, seldom practised. Talk is cheap but doing makes the difference. In this regard, character seems to be the forgotten word of our generation. To be fair, it stands little chance in the popularity stakes alongside such power words as visualisation, success, self-esteem and independence.

True character is, however, not too worried about being popular. Herein lies its strength. Character is about doing what is right, not what is necessarily convenient or well received. Character is about building an inner world that remains stable and secure, despite external concerns or comforts.

Character separates the mature from the juvenile, the champion from the mediocre, the true leaders from the masses of pretenders. Character cannot be measured by votes, record sales, congregation size or bank balance. It is both the most needed and the most underrated building block of our society. Character will enable a nation to progress economically while protecting its citizens from social disintegration. The character vacuum produced by the values, lifestyle and pace of modern living can only be filled as people begin to look within rather than without; when we begin to realize that true fulfilment and an authentic sense of significance come not from the plaudits of man, the enjoyment of life or the growth of net worth.

When the pursuit of pleasure fails and the myth of materialism becomes self-evident, the essentialness of character remains and continues to deliver its promises.

The scope and depth of the actual word, character, is hard to state simply. Most people understand and have a general feel for the meaning of the word, yet finding a workable definition that encapsulates the power and range of the idea is next to impossible.

Here, then, are a few attempts at summarizing the word, none of which are really satisfactory on their own, but when taken as a whole come closer to what character is all about:

> *'A man's reputation is only what men think him to be.*
> *His character is what God knows him to be.'*
> Joseph Addison

> *'The aggregate of features and traits that form the apparent nature of a person.'*
> Webster's Dictionary

> *'Character is simply habits, long continued.'*
> Plutarch

> *'The ability to sell the family parrot to the town gossip without fear.'*
> (Author unknown)

'*The depth and strength of the human character are defined by its moral reserves. People reveal themselves completely only when they are thrown out of the customary conditions of their life, for only then do they have to fall back on their reserves.*' [1]
Leo Trotsky

'*Who you are when no one is looking.*'
D.L. Moody

This last definition was recently experienced painfully by me. I was visiting *Ripley's Believe It or Not* museum in San Francisco. Following the walkway that led through the maze of the strange, the remarkable and the bizarre, I came to a series of booths in which there was a mirror, together with a description of how some people are specially gifted to contort their faces in unusual ways.

'One in 10,000 can touch their nose with their tongue – you try!' said the sign under the first mirror. I failed dismally and moved on to the next booth where an equally ridiculous challenge awaited.

About half an hour later, as I reached the end of my journey through the exhibits, I came to a room with a series of windows on one side and a viewing area on the other. To my delight and chagrin, I realized that these windows were the other side of the mirrors I had encountered earlier. Each was filled with an oblivious fellow traveller making a complete fool of himself, much to the delight of the assembled audience.

We humans do strange things when we think no one is watching us!

Morally, however, when we think no one is watching, our true character displays itself. What is on the inside, comes out. This comparison of inside-outside, of how who we are affects what we do, is probably the best way to build a framework for the concept of character.

The Paradigm of Being and Doing

Normally when two strangers meet, the small talk follows a standard procedure. The first question in such circumstances tends to be, 'What is your name?' Once introductions have taken place, the inevitable second stage of the relationship is to establish what the other person *does*. After all, *one is what one does*.

We are proud of our workplace accomplishments, to the degree that most of us derive our identity and self-esteem from what we do. The attendant problems of such a philosophy of life increasingly become evident. Doing takes the place of being. We become driven individuals rather than called. Our evaluation of how life is going, is totally dominated by this occupation mentality. Consequently, when retrenchment, retirement or – worse still – termination and unemployment become our lot, we lose our identity and either drop out, die, or simply become disillusioned. The cry of character would have us change our thinking about who we really are.

Character is all about being... doing is simply the reflection of our inner core. Indeed, true enjoyment in our chosen occupation is a result of doing because of being. Who I am should dictate what I do, not the other way round. In other words we are *human beings* not *human doings*!

When my external world drives me more than the dreams that are within me, I cease to be in charge. Circumstances become my compelling counsellors and the potential to become a world changer is changed by the world.

Malcolm Muggeridge states this problem forcibly and hints at an answer in his memoirs:

> *'In this Sargasso sea of fantasy and fraud how can I or anyone else hope to swim unencumbered? How see with, not through the eye? How take off my own motley, wash away the make up, raise the iron shutter, put out the studio lights, silence the sound effects and put the cameras to sleep?...*
>
> *Find furniture among the studio props, silence in a discotheque, love in a strip-tease? Read truth off an autocue, catch it on a screen, chase it on the wings of Muzak? View it in living colour with the news, hear it in living sound along the motorways? Not in the wind that rent the mountains and broke in pieces the rocks,*

not in the earthquake that followed nor in the fire that followed the earthquake. In a still small voice. Not in the screeching of tyres, neither in the grinding of brakes; nor in the roar of the jets or the whistle of sirens; not in the howl of trombones, the rattle of drums or the chanting of demo voices. Again, that still small voice – if only one could catch it.' [2]

George Bernard Shaw further illustrates this point with great clarity:

'Reasonable men adapt themselves to their environment. Unreasonable men adapt their environment to themselves; therefore all progress depends upon the efforts of unreasonable men.' [3]

When I first discovered and mulled over this quotation it greatly inspired me. We empirically understand it is all too easy, in this high pressure world, to be swept along with the tide, to march in time with the majority. We find ourselves inevitably conforming to the values, opinions and expectations of those that surround us. I believe it was this peer pressure phenomenon that Paul addressed in the New Testament when he wrote, *'Don't be conformed to this world, but be transformed by the renewing of your mind.'* [4] Our personality, character, goals and aspirations need to be fed from within rather than from without.

Inside-out living is what character is all about. Developing an inner superstructure enables us to bring power and security to our outward life. Suddenly esteem and enthusiasm for life are no longer based on the vagaries of doing, be it employment or recreation, but on the certainty of knowing who we really are on the inside. This has direct ramifications for what we do, how we do it and why we follow certain courses of actions. It is, *I am, therefore I do*, not, *I do, therefore I am*.

This type of self-analysis is incredibly difficult, as it causes us to confront the most basic of all questions, 'Who am I?'. Suddenly we discover that we have been using the doing paradigm to divert our attention away from the purpose of our own existence. We often don't want to delve into such matters for fear of what the answer holds. We have been so conditioned by the doctrines of externalism that we begin to doubt that we have anything on the inside at all. The good news, however, for those who have the courage to begin this inward journey, is that this inner world is far richer and fuller than anything we could have dreamed of. We have been, in the words of Zig Ziglar, '*endowed with the seeds of greatness*'.

Such existential living is not based on the hope that something lies within, but upon the joy and significance that comes from discovering who we really are. Developing character will cause our inner life to be strong and enable us to enjoy to the maximum, external living. Doing becomes the overflow of being and, as long as our inner self is growing and focused, our outward living will take care of itself.

The Paradigm of Inward and Outward

'As a man thinks in his heart, so is he.'[5]

Outward living should be a reflection of who we are on the inside. Unfortunately the emphasis today is very much on the public person, a job, achievements, looks and assets. Beauty is thought of in terms of physical proportions, success in terms of car model, and life in general in terms of what one has. These small ambitions envelop our focus. Character would have us major on the majors and allow the embroidery of life to follow along. Character would beseech us to develop our inner world because eventually it will reflect outward. Our focus must be on the deeper fundamental questions of meaning, purpose and spirituality. Success and achievement should be inside out. Indeed, one of the great tragedies within the Christian church is the error of many established denominations concentrating on changing people from the outside in. The Bible speaks of changing the heart, the inner attitudes, the core being of the individual, and allowing that change to work its way to the surface.

Inner growth will always relate to external growth. Who you are, whether it is the business person, parent or leader, is who you are on the inside, well before it becomes apparent on the outside. The hypocrite, of course, is the one whose inner world and outer world do not connect at all.

Many live a life of pretence, developing with great vigour a public image and yet failing to give proper attention to the heart. We are, I believe, made up of three parts: heart, mind and body. With our body we relate to the physical world; with our mind, the intellectual world; and with our heart the inner dimensions of character and spirituality. Most of us put the bulk of our energy into the mind and body. Yet to neglect the heart in order to give attention to the other realms is a decision of little insight.

Pascal's phrase, '*Pious scholars rare*',[6] probably has this in mind. What he meant, I believe, is that any individual who becomes a master in one dimension of life rarely gives time or thought to the others. Herbert Butterfield had the same truth in mind when he penned these words:

> '*Both in history and in life it is a phenomenon by no means rare, to meet with comparatively unlettered people who seem to have struck profound spiritual depths... While there are many highly educated people of whom one feels they are performing clever antics with their minds to cover a gaping hollowness that lies within.*'[7]

Character then is about what we have on the inside. In short, who we really are. This book is about exploring this inner world and learning how to develop and change our inner selves in order to experience authentic and successful living. We shall discover that, in attempting to structure our private world by building endangered character qualities, we will often need help, not only from our friends but also from God. Character it seems cannot be completely self-generated. We all need a perspective and strength greater than ourselves. We have the ability to recognize our need for change but we lack the necessary power to accomplish the task. My prayer is that as we begin to look at specific character qualities the reader will identify with the problem, decide on the solution, and reach out to the only power that can really change the hidden person of the heart.

This book is written to the person who desires to achieve and grow in life. The kind of person who is not content to simply exist, but has a sense of destiny, an inner awareness that, despite the pain of this world, they are meant to be part of the solution. The person who knows there is a job to do, and just living for the weekend and looking forward to retirement, without developing the inner resource of the heart, is the highest form of selfishness.

I believe that if we purpose to do that which is necessary to make these secrets of Super Achievers our own we will transform our lives inside and out.

We must first, however, define our terms. If definitions differ on what being a Super Achiever really is, then no doubt expectations may disappoint.

The Super Achiever cannot be defined in a mere positional or financial way. The Super Achiever is not the fabulously wealthy person, with the broken marriage, or the respected leader, caught in a prison of personal, compulsive, self-destructive habits.

The term is used holistically and covers not only our financial and career world, but also the relational, social, mental, physical and spiritual worlds. The Super Achiever is a person, not just of accomplishment, but of authentic essence and solid character. All these things are, of course, inextricably intertwined.

Most of the chapters that follow have to do with character traits which must be nurtured and developed. This is paramount to achieving our goal of success in life. Skills, techniques and practices are of secondary importance. There is a plethora of books available in today's marketplace that deal with such things. Our purpose, however, is to get at the heart of the problem and therefore to the heart of the answer... for that is where the journey begins.

14

REFERENCES

1   Leo Trotsky, *Diary in Exile*, 1959, Entry for 5 April, 1935.

2   Malcolm Muggeridge, *Chronicles of Wasted Time Vol. I*, London, Fontana, 1972, p. 19.

3   George Bernard Shaw, *Maxims for Revolutionists*, Man and Superman, 1903.

4   *New Testament Bible, Romans 12:2, NIV*, New York International Bible Society, 1978. Used by permission of Zondervan Bible Publishers.

5   *Old Testament Bible, Proverbs 23:7, KJV*, Thomas Nelson Publishers, 1982.

6   Blaise Pascal, *Pensees*, Penguin Group, 1995.

7   Herbert Butterfield, *Christianity and History*, New York, Charles Scribner's Sons, 1949, p. 115.

CHAPTER 2
JUST A PUPPET ON A STRING
Responsibility

'As human beings, we are endowed with freedom of choice, and we cannot shuffle off our responsibility upon the shoulders of God or nature. We must shoulder it ourselves. It is up to us.'

Arnold J. Toynbee

Our culture has become one of non-responsibility and complaint. Everything is someone else's fault and excuse is the morphine of our time. The legal profession has thrived on this *lie we have believed,* as our *sue-happy* society illustrates. We pay for it not only through our insurance rates but also with our souls. The teaching 'I am not to blame' has grown in popularity, especially in the last 40 years. It has been sustained by the willingness to believe, fuelled by Freudian psychology, and now fanned white hot by the genetic arguments being advanced for every type of human behaviour and misbehaviour. To be consistent then, we should never claim credit for victories won or goals achieved.

The blame mentality, if correct, would declare that nothing good or bad is ever our own fault. This type of fatalism does not wash with most people, so we moderate the harsh reality of taking it to its logical conclusion and develop an irrational philosophy of life... a philosophy that says we are the reason for our successes and others are the reason for our failures. Zig Ziglar has pointed out that we have all heard of the self-made success but never the self-made failure.

Super Achievers fight this very human tendency with every fibre of their beings. They take responsibility for their own lives. They are humble in victory, and reflective in defeat. Winston Churchill once said, '*Responsibility is the price of greatness*'. The sooner we accept that the number one person responsible for all our woes is ourself, the quicker we begin to make decisions that will change our lives.

Someone once said, '*If you could kick in the pants the person responsible for most of your troubles you wouldn't be able to sit down for a month!*'.

Time is not an endless, inevitable cycle where history repeats itself and the individual has no influence or control. Time is a line: it has a beginning and an end and it moves in a particular direction. When we live our life, it is important to understand that we are not caught in some kind of cosmic, meaningless whirlpool, where the events and circumstances we all face each day are controlling our future, and causing us to be the people we are. No! Life is more like a river. We can allow ourselves to go with the flow and see where the various currents take us, but we do have control enough to paddle to either bank or move upstream. Being responsible is to realize our choices are significant – what we do affects who we are and where we will end up. In short, our future is flexible.

An awareness of the role we play in our own lives is essential if we are to move away from the victim mentality.

John Maxwell relates in his book, *Developing the Leader Within You*,[1] some research conducted with prison inmates:

'*A psychologist asked various prisoners, "Why are you here?". The answers were very revealing, though*

*expected. There were many of them: "I was framed."
"They ganged up on me." "It was a case of mistaken
identity."*

*'The psychologist wondered, if one could possibly find
a larger group of "innocent" people anywhere else but
in prison!'*

Probably the best story I have heard illustrating the
principle of responsibility again comes from John Maxwell:

*'The sales manager of a dog food company asked his
sales people how they liked the company's new
advertising campaign.*

*'"Great. The best in the business," the sales people
responded.*

'"How do you like our new label and the package?"

*'"Great. The best in the business," the sales people
responded.*

*"How do you like our sales force?" They were the sales
force. They had to admit they were good.*

*'"OK, then," said the manager, "So we've got the best
label, the best package, the best advertising program
being sold by the best sales force in the business. Tell*

me why we are in 17th place in the dog food business?"
There was silence.

'Finally someone said, "It's those lousy dogs. They
won't eat the stuff!".' [2]

Others can slow us down or even try to put road blocks on the way to our potential, but we are the only ones that can stop the car or change direction. Super Achievers take control of their lives. They refuse to accept that their culture, heritage, net worth, physical appearance, education or lack of it, controls life. Only desire, decision and determination are important.

Four Exceptions to the Rule

There are of course some exceptions to this law of responsibility. In fact there are four:

Number One – Only Child

Only children have life pretty rough. Absence of sibling rivalry in the formative years often allows pride and self-centredness to creep in. The necessity of sharing and giving are lessons poorly learned by the only child. So when the time comes to enter the rough and tumble of life outside the domestic situation, they are ill prepared for what follows and cannot, by virtue of their upbringing, be truly successful in life.

Number Two – Middle Child

The middle child has a different set of problems to deal with. The parents boast about the oldest child and spoil the youngest, often forgetting all about the one in between. 'This is Tom our eldest, and darling Sally our youngest and this is... I'm sorry I've forgotten your name...!' The resulting inferiority complex practically guarantees the lack of achievement in the middle child's life.

Number Three – Youngest Child

The baby of the family shares many of the problems of the only child, as well as the extra pressures of parents tired of parenting, and elder brothers and sisters who resent the resulting breakdown of all previous house rules, regulations and curfews. The result is that this child lacks the ability to develop strong character in areas critical for future success and significance.

Number Four – The Eldest Child

If you thought the previous three had problems, they are nothing compared to the firstborn. Not only are they born when their parents are the least experienced, but also the most financially disadvantaged. Thus they endure parental experimentation and become the guinea pig for failure after failure. When they finally realize what is going on, the parents have a change of heart and modify all the rules for their younger brothers and sisters. It's just not fair!

My point is, one's upbringing can be used as either an excuse for failure or a reason for success. Your family, like so many others, may have been dysfunctional but we must learn to break free. We need to be mature. We need to take responsibility. Only then are we on the road to true significance.

Being responsible is to realize our choices are significant — what we do affects who we are and where we will end up. In short, our future is flexible.

REFERENCES

1   John Maxwell, *Developing the Leader Within You*, Word, 1993, p. 203.

2   Ibid, p. 205.

CHAPTER 3
DAZE OF OUR LIVES
Overriding Goal or Passion

'You will become as small as your controlling desire; or as great as your dominant aspiration.'

James Allen

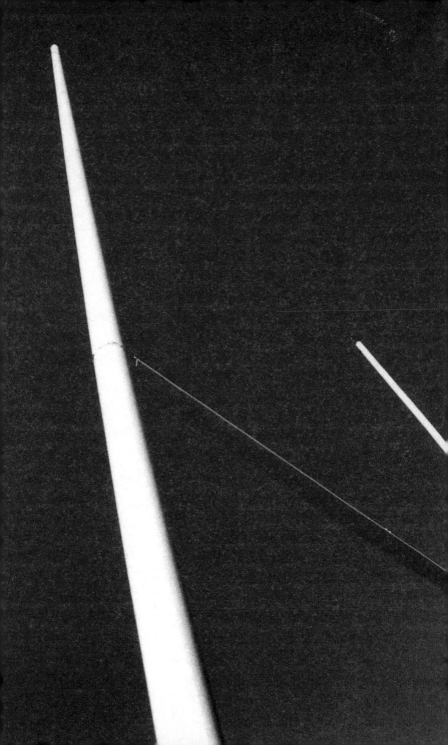

Life for the Super Achiever is not about the doing of many things, but about the accomplishing of the one thing; a direction so compelling that one could call it a life goal and within the framework of this life goal, fit all other goals. This one purpose, this one passion, gives the Super Achiever a sense of direction and a point of reference. Pursuits, desires, invitations and opportunities are all either consciously or subconsciously sifted through the perspective of the one overriding purpose.

We only have to think of the Super Achievers throughout history to realize that all of them had a singular purpose that was uppermost in their mind. Other challenges and smaller achievements accomplished in the early years were seen as preparation for the major mission.

Churchill on 10 May 1940, in the first part of World War II, became prime minister. He described it thus:

> 'I was conscious of a profound sense of relief. At last I had the authority to give directions over the whole scene. I felt as if I were walking with destiny and that all my past life had been but preparation for this hour and for this trial...'[1]

In the New Testament Paul talks about 'This one thing I do'.[2] Jesus had a single mission; to die for his people. The heart of Martin Luther King Jnr cried freedom and equality at every opportunity. Gandhi's clarion call was independence for India. Mother Teresa, and now countless disciples, are still doing her one thing, as are the countless thousands of other Super Achievers around the world.

When we, as individuals, come to terms with this truth, many of us become painfully aware, almost immediately, that we have been living fragmented lives. We attempt to move in opposite directions all at once. Floating wherever the current takes us, believing that wherever we end up will be the right destination.

The life of the Super Achiever argues against this way of thinking and their testimony is echoed by the quiet voice of our own heart. Somehow deep within us we know that if one is to reach greatness, if one is to make a difference in one's world, there must be an overall sense of direction. There must be commitment, enthusiasm and effort. There must be a willingness to go against the majority, to fight against the tides of apathy and mediocrity, to pursue with passion the reason we have been created.

Intuitively we also realize that with the discovery of our lifetime purpose there comes a general sense of contentment, fulfilment and even serenity. Pervading despair, loss of personal peace, and the overall confusion of life, are rare maladies among the Super Achievers.

The film *City Slickers* illustrates this principle. The character played by Billy Crystal, having arrived at midlife, is trying to find his smile again. Crystal and his friends decide to go on a cattle drive as a means of rediscovering themselves, where they are confronted with a simple yet penetrating truth. The old cattleman leading the muster is asked by Crystal the question, 'What is the secret of life?' and gives the answer, 'Just one thing'. When Crystal responds by asking what this *one thing* could be, the answer stops him in his tracks: 'That's what you've got to find out.'

Super Achievers have found their *one thing* and they then spend their life pursuing it with a tenacity and discipline that can only be caused by discovered destiny.

The defining call of the Super Achiever is of a far higher intensity than the regular yet ever changing plans and dreams of everyday folk.

There are certain characteristics that qualify an ambition, goal or purpose to be this *one thing*.

Bigger Than One's Self

First, it is important to have a life goal that is bigger than one's self; to have a cause that goes beyond personal wealth and satisfaction. A cause that will touch the lives of others and bring meaning to our work. It is not enough to just pay the bills, buy the Lear Jet, or to spend one's life playing golf in the world's best resorts. The idle rich have their rewards but they are nothing compared to those of the Super Achiever.

*'I am in a peculiar position. No one can give me
anything. There is nothing I want that I cannot have.
But I do not want the things that money can buy. I
want to live a life, to make the world a little better for
having lived in it.'*[3]
Henry Ford

The miser who lives for himself, dies miserably. I am
reminded of one such man who, as he reached the end
of his days, decided to try to cheat the old maxim: *You
can't take it with you.*

He summoned to his bedside his lawyer, doctor and
minister, entrusting to each an envelope containing
$100,000 cash.

'I have no friends and you gentlemen are the only ones
I can trust,' he said. 'What I have given you is the sum
total of my life's savings... I want you each to swear a
solemn pledge to throw into my grave, your envelope with
its money, as they begin to bury me.'

The three men agreed to fulfil this task and about a month
later the old miser died.

When the first clods fell onto the coffin so too did the
three envelopes as the doctor, lawyer and minister stood
seriously at the graveside. After the funeral, the three
decided to join each other for a drink. It wasn't long
before the doctor spoke up. 'Sirs, I have to confess. My

practice has been difficult, my wife has developed a serious drinking problem and money has been in short supply. I took $30,000 out of my envelope and only threw in $70,000.'

There was a moment's silence and the lawyer began to speak. 'I too must get this off my chest. These last 12 months have been very difficult for me. I have developed a gambling addiction that has almost destroyed my life. I took out $70,000 and only threw in $30,000.'

The minister, as you could well imagine, was shocked by these admissions. He stood up and addressed both men. 'Gentlemen, I cannot believe you have broken your pledges in this manner. I want you both to know that I threw in a cheque for the full amount!'

The life purpose, the goal, the consuming passion, must be something that impacts on the lives of others in a positive way.

I believe that it was this very fact that caused John Sculley, then CEO of Pepsi Company, to move to the Apple Corporation. Negotiations were failing in the attempt to entice him across to the new maverick computer firm. It was becoming apparent to Steve Jobs, one of the founders of Apple, that he could not offer Sculley anything he did not already have, especially when it came to profit sharing, salary, retirement plan or any of the perks that would go with such a position. The deal was clinched when Jobs had almost given up hope. A simple statement, 'Well, do you want to spend the rest of your life selling sugared water or do you want a chance to change the world?'… challenged Sculley to think about the bigger picture. He realized that the power of a life mission, that would impact on the world, is infinitely greater than all the possessions and respectability that money can buy.

In this light we can see why the philosophy of hedonism fails. The self-absorbed life, the life intent upon personal pleasure as its primary goal, will always lead to disillusionment and finally despair.

The self-obsessed life cannot lead to inner meaning, serenity or any sense of significance. The lie of our culture is that a *me first* philosophy is the key to success. However, even a cursory look at what brings prosperity and achievement in any endeavour in life begins to show that self-absorption is a sure path to failure.

A sporting team must work together as a team, serving one another. A business needs to harness power through synergy. A good leader must serve those he is called to lead. Christ, of course, was the ultimate example of putting others first. Not only by his death but also in his lifestyle: he taught that honouring God and loving people is the key to one's own fruitfulness and fulfilment. When seen in this light, success comes to those who use it to bless others. Success is God's way of helping other people. The business person who is trying to be successful just for himself will never compare with the one who has a bigger goal: the goal to reach out and touch the lives of others.

We are wired up to find our greatest fulfilment and joy in using who we are and what we have to benefit those around us. It has been truly said, that one quickly finds the falseness of materialism or hedonism by attempting to live them out. Those who give their lives to philanthropy and service, discover they are living life at its deepest and most rewarding level.

You Love It!

> *'Your chances of success are directly proportional to the degree of pleasure you derive from what you do. If you are in a job you hate, face the fact squarely and get out.'*
> Michael Korda

One of the brightest signposts to destiny is love. Often the decision to change career paths from the well-paying but unenjoyable job, to a riskier endeavour that fires the soul, opens the way for unrealized potential.

Isaac Asimov, the science fiction writer, is a case in point. Leaving the secure position of college professor, he became one of the most successful writers of modern times, with over 470 books published.

Vincent Van Gogh, who left Christian ministry to paint, simply because he loved it, in one of his letters makes this point clearly:

> 'In my opinion, I am often rich as Croesus – not in money, but (though it doesn't happen every day) rich – because I have found in my work, something which I can devote myself to heart and soul, and which inspires me and gives a meaning to life.' [4]

It has been well said that most die with their music still in them. Probably because they never gave themselves wholeheartedly to what they loved to do or, worse still, that love eluded them all their lives.

Love and destiny go hand in hand. We are wired with both purpose and passion. When we discover one, we will find the other.

Discovered – Not Chosen

> 'I refuse to believe the notion that man is flotsam and jetsam in the river of life, unable to respond to the eternal forever that confronts him.'
> Dr Martin Luther King Jnr

A third characteristic of the type of goal that can re-orientate an entire life, is that it is discovered rather than chosen. Intuition here is far more important than analysis.

We must look deep within the recesses of our soul to find out why we have been made. What gets me excited? What gets me angry? What do I dream about? What would I do if I could do anything? If I knew it was impossible for me to fail, what would I attempt? What gifts and talents do I have, even in an embryonic stage, which if developed to their potential could make a difference to this world?

Life goals almost have a sense of predestination about them. When people finally reach the point when they say, 'This is what I choose to do with my life', they are also aware that somehow their life was chosen to do this. They find, as a result, that they are not driving themselves towards a goal but are operating out of a deep sense of call.

Churchill's words, quoted earlier, give us the impression that when he found his life's purpose he was aware, at the deepest level, that he was not deciding to do this but that the decision had already been made. He was meant to do this. This revelation may have come to him in a sudden flash, a eureka moment, and in his case, late in life. On the other hand it may have developed as a deep sense of knowing from an early age. Regardless of how one comes to the understanding of our purpose, it is vitally important that we believe that there is such a purpose, and that we spend our lives looking, asking and expecting its sudden or slow arrival. Perhaps it may even be, while reading these very words, you find a deep stirring within your heart, a realization that you have been satisfied with the status quo and settled for mediocrity. The time has come to be desperate enough to search, find and follow the dream of your heart and the intended purpose of your soul.

The self-absorbed life, the life intent upon personal pleasure as its primary goal, will always lead to disillusionment and finally despair.

REFERENCES

1   Martin Gilbert. *'Winston S Churchill'* , *The Second World War Vol. 2*, London, Heinemann, 1949, p. 10.

2   *New Testament Bible, Philippians 3:13, KJV*, Thomas Nelson Publishers, 1982.

3   Samuel S. Marquis, *Henry Ford: An Interpretation*, Boston, Little, Brown & Co., 1923.

4   Bruce Bernard, *Vincent by Himself*, Boston, Little, Brown & Co., 1985, p. 43.

CHAPTER 4
YOU HAVE TO JUMP IN THE PUDDLES
Optimism

'The higher you go in any organization of value, the better the attitude you'll find.'

John Maxwell

Super Achievers tend to be highly optimistic people. Not only do they believe in others, but their view of life is that things are somehow going to work out their way. This perspective pervades every part of their being.

Optimism is all about having a positive outlook, maintaining a sense of humour, and developing long term hope.

Positive Outlook

Helen Keller declared, '*life is a daring adventure or it is nothing*'. The Super Achievers would agree. They tend naturally to see the best rather than the worst. They are the kind of people who are genuinely disappointed when their lottery ticket doesn't win (although they don't usually buy lottery tickets).

A positive outlook is more than smiling in the face of problems or simplistically pretending that things are not as bad as they really are. Optimism is a deep inner belief that, despite everything, there is more going for you than against you. That love, hope, integrity, while not always appearing to win through in the external circumstances of life, build an inner strength that far outshines the alternative. '*Without minimising catastrophe, the consistent and astonishing result is that the worst emotional consequences of bad events are usually temporary,*'[1] writes social psychologist, David G. Myers.

His comment is based on the attitude and inner world of the one suffering. The ability to look beyond the immediate and search for the positive is the surest and speediest path to both recuperation and growth. Myers continues by citing the example of W. Mitchell:

> *'In 1971, he was horribly burned, nearly killed and left fingerless from a freak motorcycle accident. Four years later tragedy struck again. This time he was paralysed from the waist down in a small plane crash. Though terribly disfigured he chose not to buy the idea that happiness requires handsomeness. "I am in charge of my own spaceship. It is my up, my down. I could choose to see this situation as a setback or a starting point." Mitchell today is a successful investor, an environmental activist, and a speaker who encourages people to step back from their own misfortunes: "Take a wider view and say: Maybe this isn't such a big thing after all!"'* [2]

Dark pessimism, as a philosophy of life, leads to despair, depression and cynicism. Those that take this perspective fail to see, much less admire, the rainbows of life. Their attention is on the storm. Denis Waitley says, *'Losers see icy streets but winners put on ice skates'*. The pessimist's light at the end of the tunnel is the oncoming train and his stubborn refusal to believe anything else locks him into a vicious cycle of self-fulfilling prophecy.

Optimism, however, still grits the teeth at life's difficulties but does so with a slight smile on the face.

It has been said, '*The trials of life will either wear you down, or polish you up, depending on what you are made of*'. Those who are negative in life only see the problems. When opportunity knocks they complain about the noise. Their glass of water is half empty because they are draining the water away. The optimist on the other hand is solution conscious. They are adding to the water level and excited about the future. They are quick to follow Henry Ford's dictum, '*Don't find fault, find a remedy*'.

The Super Achiever in life is hardly ever the sombre, intense, overly melancholic individual. Rather, he or she tends to have a sparkle in the eye, a skip in their step, and a sense of play and wonder.

In this, we can learn a lot from children. Indeed, we can learn a lot from ourselves when we were children. Remember laughing out loud at everyday occurrences which now we don't even notice. Remember jumping in puddles when it rained and being careful not to walk on the cracks?

I think, as adults we should jump in more puddles rather than complain about the rain. We should sing more, smile more and take time to smell the flowers, look at the view and enjoy the journey.

We rush lemming-like through life, frustrated at red lights, impatient in elevators and hassled by the queues. Life will always have its puddles and red lights, but they are there to be enjoyed; welcome distractions and breaks in the rush hour of life.

While I am writing this, I am sitting at a street cafe; the rain has started to fall, much to the delight of a small, two-year-old girl. She is standing outside, face upward, trying to catch a few raindrops in her mouth, and I... I am upset that my notes are getting wet!

Optimism in one sense doesn't change anything but, in another, changes everything. Life is not about what happens to you but how you react to it. The Super Achiever realizes there is always something in life to be thankful for. The serious view of life, even if it may be more realistic at times, is not as much fun, and fun is necessary to sabotage stress, diffuse frustration and maximize productiveness.

Sense of Humour

Ogden Nash once wrote:

> 'It is better in the long run to possess an abscess or a tumour than to possess a sense of humour.
> 'People who have senses of humour have a very good time
> 'But they never accomplish anything of note – either despicable or sublime.

*'Because how can anybody accomplish anything
immortal
'When they realize they look pretty funny doing it and
have to stop and chortle?'*[3]

Ogden Nash was wrong!

While great leaders in any area are rarely comedians, they do share the ability to laugh at life and themselves. Being able to see the funny side is often what enables the Super Achiever to endure with grace and move smoothly through life's difficult spots. Humour is the oil that reduces the friction of great responsibility.

Churchill is one of my favourites in this regard. There are several well-known stories that illustrate this principle in his life.

During the war years as prime minister he was lauded for his speeches, but not by all. A certain woman backbencher took much delight in continually interjecting her disagreements with him. In one particular speech she called out, 'If you were my husband I would poison your tea'. To which Winston responded, 'And if you were my wife, I would drink it!'.

On another occasion, George Bernard Shaw sent Churchill a letter containing tickets. The letter read:

'Dear Winston
Please find enclosed two tickets to the opening night of
my new play, "St Joan".
PS: Please bring a friend… if you have one!'

Churchill returned the tickets the following day with a
letter of his own.

'Dear Bernard
Sorry, unable to make the opening night of your new
play.
PS: Please send tickets for second night… if there is
one!'

Religious people have a tendency to be intense, serious
and often lacking in humour. The Pharisees who accosted
Jesus were such individuals. Yet those that walk with God
in an authentic way are quick to smile. No wonder Malcolm
Muggeridge entitled his biography of Mother Teresa,
Something Beautiful for God.

A vibrant sense of humour is an attribute of God himself.
Laughing during life's journey improves the view and
reduces the stress. James Thurber wrote:

'Humour is counterbalance. Laughter need not be cut
out of anything, since it improves everything. The
power that created the poodle, the platypus and people
has an integrated sense of both comedy and tragedy.' [4]

Sense of Hope

The loss of hope is the problem of our age. Progressively the foundations of society have been undermined... hope is the last to fall. One unknown author put it this way:

'In the 1950s, kids lost their innocence. They were liberated from their parents by well-paying jobs, cars, and lyrics in music that gave rise to a new term – the generation gap.

'In the 1960s, kids lost their authority. It was the decade of protest – church, state and parents were all called into question and found wanting. Their authority was rejected, yet nothing ever replaced it.

'In the 1970s, kids lost their love. It was the decade of me-ism, dominated by hyphenated words beginning with self: self-image, self-esteem, self-assertion. It made for a lonely world. Kids learned everything there was to know about sex but forgot everything there was to know about love, and no one had the nerve to tell them the difference.

'In the 1980s, kids lost their hope. Stripped of innocence, authority and love, and plagued by the horror of a nuclear nightmare, large and growing numbers of their generation stopped believing in the future.' [5]

Hope is essential for life itself. Despair leads to death. This is why the words at the entrance to hell in Dante's inferno: '*All hope abandon, ye who enter here*', are so damning.

The Super Achiever not only maintains hopes, but usually has an active plan to develop them. He or she believes in getting their hopes up. Such hope in life, in the future, is an absolute prerequisite to successful endeavour in any field. Even in the pragmatic area of economics, the power of hope, with its legitimate child, faith, cannot be undervalued. As George Gilder, writer for the Wall Street Journal, points out:

> *'Faith in man, faith in the future, faith in the rising returns of giving, faith in the mutual benefits of trade, faith in the providence of God, are all essential to successful capitalism. All are necessary to sustain the spirit of work and enterprise against the setbacks and frustrations it inevitably meets in a fallen world; to inspire trust and cooperation in an economy where they will often be betrayed; to encourage the forgoing of present pleasures in the name of a future that may well go up in smoke; to promote risk and initiative in a world where the rewards all vanish unless others join the game. In order to give without the assurance of return, in order to save without the certainty of future value, in order to work beyond the requirements of the job, one has to have confidence in a higher morality: a law of compensations beyond the immediate and distracting struggles of existence.'* [6]

There is a dimension to hope we don't often think about. That is a sense of hope that is produced not by the expectation of a favourable outcome, but rather by the sense of purpose in what we are doing, regardless of outcome.

Vaclav Havel, the brilliant and compassionate President of the Czech Republic, has seen this, better than most. For many years he was an opposition writer whose protestations in the name of human rights landed him in jail several times. In the face of an all-controlling communism, he held on to hope because he was convinced not of the final victory his ideas would have, but simply because they were right and true:

> 'I should probably say first that the kind of hope I often think about (especially in situations that are particularly hopeless, such as prison) I understand above all as a state of mind, not a state of the world. Either we have hope within us or we don't; it is a dimension of the soul and it's not essentially dependent on some particular observation of the world or estimate of the situation. Hope is not prediction...

> 'Hope, in this deep and powerful sense, is not the same as joy that things are going well, or willingness to invest in enterprises that are obviously headed for success, but rather an ability to work for something because it is good, not just because it stands a chance to succeed. The more unfavourable the situation in

*which we demonstrate hope, the deeper that hope is.
Hope is definitely not the same thing as optimism. It is
not the conviction that something will turn out well,
but the certainty that something makes sense,
regardless of how it turns out.*' [7]

Probably the best known example of such remarkable hope was recorded by Victor Frankl. His book, *Man's Search for Meaning* was a product of the Nazi concentration camps. Dr Frankl spent three years as a prisoner in four different camps and observed and felt the extremities of human suffering.

He discovered the only thing that kept the condemned alive was hope. *'He who has a "why" can live with almost any "how".'*

It was this *why* that gave rise to the hope that sustained life in its darkest hour.

Frankl recounts an address he gave to a group of fellow prisoners on this very point:

*'I asked the poor creatures, who listened to me
attentively in the darkness of the hut, to face the
seriousness of our position. They must not lose hope
but should keep their courage in the certainty that the
hopelessness of our struggle did not detract from its
dignity and its meaning. I said that someone looks
down on each of us in difficult hours – a friend, a*

wife, somebody alive or dead, or a God – and he would not expect us to disappoint him. He would hope to find us suffering proudly – not miserably – knowing how to die.[8]

Hope can begin to dissipate simply through the process of ageing and thus cannot be simply taken for granted. We must work to keep our hopes up.

Every time I go to a funeral, I am confronted with the inevitable end of the mortal road. It never used to grab me, but now as the years roll by, I begin to sense its presence. It seems the older the person the sadder we are at such occasions. We mourn for ourselves and the deceased. We bid adieu to one who has finished, with the inescapable knowledge that one day it will be us, our time will come and young men and women will follow our casket and then return to their lives. For them, their day is far away... as it was once for us.

It is not only possible but essential to build hope as we get older. This may seem difficult in the face of such an inescapable conclusion as death. Still, there is one who came back from the other side and my faith, love and hope are founded upon him.

REFERENCES

1   David Myers, *The Pursuit of Happiness*, Aquarium Press, 1993, p. 48.

2.   Ibid, p. 49.

3   Ogden Nash, *Don't Grin or You'll Have to Bear It, I'm a Stranger Here Myself*, 1938.

4   James Thurber, *Letter to Frances Glennon*, June, 1959.

5   Author unknown, quoted in *A Shattered Visage, The Real Face of Atheism*, Ravi Zacharias, Baker Book House, 1990, p. 103.

6   George Gilder, *Wealth and Poverty*, ICS Press, 1993, p. 84.

7   Vaclav Havel, *Disturbing the Peace*, New York Vintage, 1991, p. 181, as quoted by David Aikman, *Hope: The Heart's Greatest Quest*, Servant Publications, 1995, p. 11.

8   Victor Frankl, *Man's Search for Meaning*, London, Hodder and Stoughton, 1964, p. 83.

CHAPTER 5
FATAL DISTRACTION
Focus

'Every great man has become great, every successful man has succeeded, in proportion as he has confined his powers to one particular channel.'

Orison Swett Marden

Super Achievers have learned the importance
and concentration and refuse to be led away on inter
yet fatal distractions.

> *'Racing is all I want to do. I don't have a Plan A and
> a Plan B.'*
> Mario Andretti

Chet Atkins, member of the country music hall of fame,
puts it this way:

> *'Maybe there are a few shortcuts for a rock star who
> becomes an overnight sensation and is forgotten about
> tomorrow. But you take a guy like Glen Campbell,
> who's a very good guitarist, or Ray Clark, a great
> entertainer, or Jerry Reed. They spent twelve hours a
> day for many years playing the guitar. They may tell
> you different, but they did. Everybody does. I took the
> guitar with me to the bathroom, everywhere I went, I
> played it – because I loved it. Jerry Reed says, "You
> gotta be eat up with it! You've got to love it with a
> passion that will follow you to the grave… If you don't
> have that, you might as well forget it, I think."'* [1]

The realization of one's life goal is all important. It is
both primary and paramount in becoming a Super
Achiever because from this discovery flow the other
characteristics required to reach our potential. The first
result in discovering our calling, as it were, is that we find
our life becomes focused. The capacity to concentrate

on the important things rather than the superficial is a direct result of knowing where one is going. Focus enables us to control our consciousness, to guard our heart and to protect our mind. We must have such protection against causes, ambitions and other fascinations, which may not be harmful in the final analysis but by their very existence cause us to get sidetracked and lose momentum.

The ability to concentrate always brings results. Whether we are talking about concentrating on an exam, in a negotiation process or upon winning the love of our life... concentration yields fruit. Such focus harnesses all our powers at once. Zig Ziglar gives the analogy of holding a magnifying glass, in the heat of the day, over a pile of dry leaves. While we keep moving the magnifying glass, we will never create the heat necessary to start the fire. The moment we hold it stationary, allowing the light and heat of the sun to focus on one small part of the foliage, the leaves will quickly burst into flame.

Why is it that a life of focus brings such great rewards? There are two major reasons. One has to do with motivation; the other with simplicity.

Motivation

First of all, focus unleashes the necessary motivation that moves us towards our life mission. There should be no surprise regarding the fact that success in life is all about such things as attitude, consistency, character and motivation. Without such traits, the competent, the able and the genius will fall far behind. William Ward put it this way:

> *'Enthusiasm and persistence can make an average person superior. Indifference and lethargy can make a superior person average.'*

Simple laziness is all too often unfairly blamed. Lethargy is more a symptom, not a cause of failure in life. My favourite quote on the subject of laziness is by Spike Milligan:

> *'Well we can't stand around here doing nothing, people will think we are workmen.'* [2]

The truth is, however, most people are not lazy, they are simply uninspired. Motivation comes from having a goal that is inspirational. This, in turn, causes us to focus our lives even more and gives us the energy through which we can accomplish our dreams.

> *'The goal becomes both the target and the fuel.'* [3]

Not all motivation is necessarily good motivation. There are several different types:

Fear Motivation

This is motivation in its lowest form. Fear motivation involves doing something because we don't like the consequences of not doing it. It is often used by parents to motivate children, and teachers their pupils. Employers have attempted to use it with questionable results. 'Firings will continue until morale improves!' Fear motivation works for a little while, but will usually produce such side products as resentment and bitterness and is, at best, effective only over the short term.

I am reminded of a man who tried to lose weight by using this type of motivation. He called it the blackmail diet! He created fear motivation for himself by placing all his savings into a trust account that would be payable to a Neo-Nazi party if he did not lose 20 kilos by the end of the year. The dread of losing his money, and giving it to an organization he despised was sufficient motivation to reach his goal...

Incentive Motivation

The next level of motivation is incentive motivation. This involves doing something because of the rewards that become ours, when we do it.

'Whoever reaches the number one spot this month will be sent on an all expenses paid holiday to Bali'; 'If you tidy your room tonight you can sit up and watch an extra half hour of television', are both examples of incentive motivation. The old carrot in front of the donkey does seem to get things done. The problem arises, however, when the donkey gets bored with the carrot or simply has had enough to eat.

Internal Motivation

The third type is the highest form of motivation... This involves doing something because we want to do it, despite the penalties of not doing it or the rewards for achieving it. This is an energy that comes from within and moves us forward. We achieve because we believe. We have it within ourselves to get the job done.

I hesitate to stoop to such a crass example, but in the film Rocky III, Rocky decides to get his title back, not because of the loss of respect or for financial rewards, but simply because he wants it for himself. He is thus enabled to face his fears and come out of the bout having won the inner fight – self-respect intact.

One key secret of the Super Achievers is that they have this kind of motivation. They keep on knocking on the doors when everyone else has given up. They have a stubbornness that goes beyond the norm and the ability to believe they will get the job done, because somehow they are meant to. This knowing that they are meant to, motivates them from the inside out.

Simplicity

> *'I have only one purpose, the destruction of Hitler, and my life is much simplified, thereby. If Hitler invaded Hell, I would make at least a favourable reference to the Devil in the House of Commons.'* [4]
> Winston Churchill

The focused life also enables maximum energy and time to be put towards the primary goal. The focused world automatically simplifies itself to fulfil the task at hand.

So often, those who do not achieve in life are wasting time and energy in the multiplicity of tasks and pursuits. This type of approach normally results in mediocrity or at best, mere competence. Excellence, however, belongs to those who would do nothing else. The Super Achiever refuses to allow the urgent to replace the important.

Simplicity enables us to know what we should overlook. This planned neglect of things outside our field of vision can and will yield great reward.

> *'He who seeks one thing, and but one,*
> *May hope to achieve it before life is done.*
> *But he who seeks all things wherever he goes,*
> *Must reap around him in whatever he sows*
> *A harvest of barren regret.'* [5]

The ability to *'lay aside every weight... that we may run the race'* [6] is a direct result of a focused life. The Super Achiever realizes that diversions may be interesting in their own right but the sidetrack they inevitably present will simply delay or even destroy the sense of direction and commitment that is central to the road of significance. Such simplicity helps us make full use of our allotted time.

Benjamin Franklin said, *'Dost thou love life? Then do not squander time because that is the stuff life is made of.'* Kennedy declared, *'We must use time as a tool not as a couch.'* [7]

The focused life, then, is both a simple life (in the sense of direction) and a motivated one. Weeks may pass with few visible results but momentum is building and, inevitably, destiny will become reality.

REFERENCES

1   As told to Eugene Griessman, *The Achievement Factors*, New York, Dodd, Mead & Co., 1987, p. 145.

2   Goon Show, BBC Radio, 1959.

3   Denis Waitley, Public Lecture, Wellington, New Zealand, 1986.

4   Winston Churchill, *The Grand Alliance, Who Said What When*, London, Bloomsbury Publications, 1988, p. 249.

5   R Earl Allen, *Let It Begin in Me*, Nashville, Broadnen Press, 1985, as quoted by John Maxwell, *Developing the Leader Within You*, p. 47.

6   *New Testament Bible, Hebrews 12:1, NIV*, New York International Bible Society, 1978. Used by permission of Zondervan Bible Publishers.

7   'Observer', Sayings of the Week, 10 December, 1961.

CHAPTER 6
IT'S NOT CHECK OUT TIME YET
Endurance

'Never, never, never, never

give up.'

Winston Churchill

Achieving in life is not just being in the right place at the right time, but also being in the wrong place at the wrong time and not giving up. Greatness is often born in the cauldron of suffering and pain, where the abilities to maintain perspective and walk in forgiveness are learned. It is in the hard places, the lonely places, that we discover if we really have an all-consuming purpose or sense of destiny.

Super Achievers respond to pain differently from other people. They do not look for escape, but for lessons. They get better rather than bitter. They realize that, in the words of Robert Schuller, *'Tough times don't last, tough people do.'* More than that, they see pain and trial as prerequisites for the character lessons that must be learned if destiny is to be reached. Churchill learned patience and persistence in his wilderness years between the wars. Kennedy's suffering at the Bay of Pigs, when the plan to depose Castro came unstuck, was the right kind of preparation for the Cuban Missile Crisis.

The achievement of one's goal in life does not come at a discounted price. Many refuse to pay it. The Super Achiever, however, the leader, realizes that before victory there is battle; before resurrection, a cross. You cannot have one without the other.

William Penn once said, *'No pain, no palm; no thorns, no throne; no gall, no glory; no cross, no crown.'* Helen Keller, who certainly had her fair share of pain and problems, wrote, *'Character cannot be developed in ease and quiet. Only through experience of trial and suffering can the soul be strengthened, vision cleared, ambition inspired and success achieved.'*[1]

It would be wrong to surmise from the preceding paragraphs that our reaction to tests should be one of acceptance and passivity. The very word *endurance* has in it the concept of fighting and resisting. A stoical attitude to life may be effective against anxiety but it does not, at the same time, achieve destiny. No – for that, one must cling to the dream and with every fibre of one's being, go to the battle. Hamlet's soliloquy brilliantly contrasts the active versus the passive view of overcoming obstacles:

> *'To be or not to be. That is the question. Whether 'tis nobler in the mind to suffer the slings and arrows of outrageous fortune or to take arms against a sea of troubles and by opposing, end them.'* [2]

We must *'not go gentle into that good night'*, we must *'Rage, rage against the dying of the light'*, [3] and we must fight for the good things and the great things.

No one ever said reaching destiny and making a difference were easy tasks.

Swimming upstream is never simple and yet the more one does it, the more natural it becomes. Muscles are developed,

new territory is reached and the joy of fulfilling our
potential suffuses our life.

In one study of successful people from different walks of
life it was discovered the problems they had faced were
more severe, not less severe, than the average person.
One quarter had major handicaps such as deafness,
blindness or crippled limbs. Three quarters had either
come from broken homes or been born in abject poverty.

The common thread to all their lives was that their
problems simply built an even stronger determination to
overcome. They chose an attitude of responsibility and
learning, refusing to bow down to the victim mentality.

The majority, of course, decide not to live this way or
simply just don't decide. The currents of negativity and
pressure will then invariably sweep the marriage, the
business or the life downstream to mediocrity or ruin.
That is not the way for us. We must have and hold on to
a different spirit if we are to continue on the road to our
significance. Upstream is better, not worse, and the
benefits of such a life are discovered enroute.

I like what a matador once said about the hazards of his
profession:

> *'I'm glad that bulls have horns because, if they didn't,*
> *I wouldn't get paid very much!'*

This compares with the lion tamer who put this advertisement in the paper. 'Lion Tamer wants tamer lion!'

Enduring the Storm

Here then are some practical principles to help endure in the midst of a storm.

Number One – Realize Storms Never Last

When all is black and destiny seems lost, a shift in the wind can cause things to quickly turn around.

Time itself is a great change agent and healer. What today seems unsurmountable and impenetrable can tomorrow be nothing but ruins. This is why it is important not to get out of the train in the middle of a tunnel.

Gandhi's words, which producer Sir Richard Attenborough highlighted in his film about the Indian leader, show how this truth kept Gandhi moving forward towards his destiny:

> *'When I despair, I remember that all through history the way of truth and love has always won. There have been tyrants and murderers and for a time they can seem invincible, but in the end they always fall... always...'*

The poet Shelley is maybe most famous for his poem
'Ozymandias', which reminds us how even the mightiest
eventually pass away:

> *'I met a traveller from an ancient land*
> *Who said: Two vast and trunkless legs of stone*
> *Stand in the desert... Near them, on the sand,*
> *Half sunk, a shattered visage lies, whose frown,*
> *And wrinkled lip, and sneer of cold command,*
> *Tell that its sculptor well those passions read*
> *Which yet survive, stamped on these lifeless things,*
> *The hand that mocked them and the heart that fed*
> *And on the pedestal these words appear:*
> *"My name is Ozymandias, king of kings:*
> *Look on my works, ye Mighty, and despair!"*
> *Nothing beside remains. Round the decay*
> *Of that colossal wreck, boundless and bare*
> *The lone and level sands stretch far away.'*

Number Two – Resource Yourself

Abraham Lincoln once said, *'Success is going from failure
to failure without loss of enthusiasm.'*

The ability to maintain such enthusiasm when all is dark,
divides between life's leaders and responders. When
circumstances in life deplete our energy reserves, we must
learn how to resource ourselves. Loss of emotional fuel
can and will be fatal on the journey.

Where does this energy come from? I believe there are two major sources:

FRIENDS

Great friends come into their own in the tough times. This is why the value of friendship cannot be overstated. Samuel Johnson put it this way:

> *'To let friendship die away by negligence and silence is certainly not wise. It is voluntarily to throw away one of the greatest comforts of this weary pilgrimage.'*

In times of trouble a true friend is concerned with helping and challenging, not just commiserating. Now is not the time to have coffee with those who will sympathize and make you feel sorry for yourself. Now is the time to draw strength and encouragement from those who will fan the glowing embers of hope. Remember the pity party can easily lead to the *last rites*.

The flip side to this coin is, however, that the Super Achiever must have a resource even beyond friends. There are times when we are all alone, totally deserted. If at these times, we must have others, input or approval to make it, we will fail.

We will, of course, never have everybody's approval. The realization of this early in life is a major key to forging ahead. It was Bill Cosby who reminded us of the old quote,

'I don't know what the secret of success is, but the secret of failure is trying to please everybody.'[4]

This idea of keeping everybody happy is something that seems to be deeply ingrained within us. We want to please others by being the type of person that they want us to be. There comes a point, however, when such living shows itself up as inauthentic. The resulting loss of significance and the increase of stress in our lives are both symptoms of trying to be somebody else's man or woman. This cognitive dissonance begins to erode the very fabric of our soul. At best we learn to live without fulfilling who we really are. At worst, we become victims, emotionally destroyed and easily manipulated.

Dr Chris Thurman states:

'If you feel you have to have everyone's approval, I want you to do something that purposely proves that you can survive without it. Go yell out the time in the middle of a large store. Walk down the street wearing Mickey Mouse ears. Express a different opinion in a conversation at work tomorrow. If someone asks you to do something that you feel is an unfair request, say no. I am not encouraging you to do anything unkind, immoral or dangerous, I am just encouraging you to act in a manner that is consistent with the truth – you can't please everyone. Don't be surprised that life will go on, because it will.'[5]

Sometimes then, we persevere with the aid and love of our friends, but we must be able to continue alone if we desire to follow in the path of the Super Achiever.

There are times when there is no human we can share the anguish with, yet perspective and strength must be obtained. The answer lies, I believe, in connecting in some way with God.

SUPERNATURAL ENERGY

Throughout history humanity has realized this hard truth: that loneliness is the companion to pain.

Ella Wheeler Wilcox in her poem, 'Solitude', makes this point well:

> *'Laugh, and the world laughs with you;*
> *Weep, and you weep alone;*
> *For the sad old earth must borrow its mirth,*
> *But has trouble enough of its own.*
> *Sing and the hills will answer;*
> *Sigh, it is lost on the air;*
> *The echoes bound to a joyful sound,*
> *But shrink from voicing care.*
>
> *'Rejoice, and men will seek you;*
> *Grieve, and they turn and go;*
> *They want full measure of all your pleasure,*
> *But they do not need your woe.*

Be glad and your friends are many;
Be sad, and you lose them all –
There are none to decline your nectared wine,
But alone you must drink life's gall.

'Feast, and your halls are crowded;
Fast, and the world goes by.
Succeed and give, and it helps you live,
But no man can help you die.
There is room in the halls of pleasure;
For a large and lordly train,
But one by one we must all file on
Through the narrow aisles of pain.'

Yet all is not lost. The human soul has inner reservoirs of strength that may be released when we begin to look beyond ourselves, to our God.

Jesus, all alone on the cross; King David when his own troops began to turn on him; Margaret Thatcher, during the time of the Brighton Bomb; Cromwell during the civil war; Churchill in his wilderness years...

God desires to be *'A present help in time of trouble'.*[6] Yet we only begin to receive such help when we come to the end of ourselves and look upward with humility and faith.

This idea of receiving help from God is for many like cheating in a game of cards. 'Life is tough,' they mutter.

'We should not be looking for theological morphine to dull the pain of reality.'

So, is faith in God merely a crutch for weak minds and cowardly souls? Or, on the other hand, is atheism a crutch for those who cannot face the reality of God?

> *'When one attempts to live without God, the answers to morality, hope and meaning send one back into his or her own world to fashion an individualised answer. Living without God means lifting oneself up by his or her own metaphysical bootstraps, whichever way is chosen... living without God is also making an absolute commitment to a philosophy of life's essence and destiny which, if wrong, affords absolutely no recourse should it be proven false. That is the degree of faith required of one who espouses an antitheistic lifestyle...*

> *'Can man live without God? Of course he can, in a physical sense. Can he live without God in a reasonable way? The answer to that is No! Because such a person is compelled to deny a moral law, to abandon hope, to forfeit meaning, and to risk no recovery if he is wrong. Life just offers too much evidence to the contrary.'* [7]

Many, sometime in life, reach this point when it is just them and God. Well-cemented atheism or fundamentalist pride are quickly dissolved at such moments. Decisions are made within the heart that either reach out the hand to him or shun his beckoning. The choice is ours and yet if we turn our backs, the shaft of light, which briefly illuminated our soul, disappears quickly into the fog of our own pride and problems.

Number Three – Hang in There

It is always encouraging to me to learn how many of the world's Super Achievers were average people who simply would not give up or let go of the dream.

We can easily make the mistake of thinking that successful people just get out there and succeed. In reality they just get out there and stay there through failure after failure. The law of percentages slowly begins to work in their favour and finally the home run is hit, the manuscript is accepted, the business finds its niche, or the vote is won.

Helen Gurley Brown, for many years editor of *Cosmopolitan* in America, comments: *'One of the most common mistakes people make in their careers is that they "check out too soon". They don't want to do the grubby stuff. They want to get to the top too quickly.'*[8]

Helen Brown is a good example of the persistence and tenacity required to reach the top as she progressively worked her way up through the organization. The willingness to do virtually any job and excel she calls *mouse burgering*, because in the beginning, the novice may feel as insignificant as a tiny mouse.[9]

Probably the best encapsulation of this truth is Zig Ziglar's quip, *'The only difference between the big shot and the little shot, is that the big shot was simply the little shot that kept on shooting.'*

It is one thing to have a life purpose, but without this sense of tenacity, dogged determination and never giving up, the dream can quickly become the fantasy. We enjoy it in our imagination, in the idle moments of life, but we will never see its birth into the real world.

In the final analysis, raw talent is not enough, yet simple tenacity will make the difference. From Lincoln to Lindberg, from Franklin to Ford, from Cromwell to Cousteau, the determination never to give up was the chief aid on the pathway to success. We must learn how to face defeat without being defeated.

Super Achievers have had more than their fair share of disappointments, but never live with the regret of giving up. They know how to tough it out, play hurt, grit their teeth and keep on.

Griessman tells of an interview he had with the legendary singer, Ray Charles:

> *'"When the crowd's with you, it does something for you."*

'"And what do you do," I asked, "When the crowd is small and isn't with you?"

'He paused… "That's when you find out whether you're a pro or not… You can't let yourself get down. If you're able to drag on stage, you've gotta be true to thyself. I must be true to Ray."' [10]

I personally love what the actor Bob Hoskins said, when asked about his consistent self-confidence in the face of discouragement and criticism:

'My Mum said to me very early – "Son if they don't like you, they've got bad taste."'

Number Four – Remember Your Dream

Remember your dream. Often, as we contemplate the history of our inner revelation of purpose and destiny, the temptation to let it go will dissipate.

Remembering these key moments of inspiration and direction is fundamental to continuing the journey. Such watersheds in our human experience should be well marked so that we can return to the spot and gain energy for the future.

Successful cultures and organizations build traditions around important milestones for this very reason.

The Jewish Passover not only illustrates with powerful symbolism the deliverance from the oppression that the people of Israel suffered, but speaks to them anew each year of the unique place they have in the eyes of God and human history.

Tradition, a knowledge of history, even nostalgia, can all play a part in moving us forward.

As a minister, when everything within me wants to throw in the towel, I begin to remember my time of calling and, as I do, a gradual strength and assurance begins to build in my heart.

So when disaster, disappointment or disability moves in on the Super Achiever, rather than leaving the race, they become servants of a greater destiny.

> 'Cripple him and you have a Sir Walter Scott. Lock him in a prison cell, and you have a John Bunyon. Bury him in the snows of valley forge, and you have a George Washington. Raise him in abject poverty and you have an Abraham Lincoln. Strike him down with infantile paralysis and he becomes Franklin Roosevelt. Burn him so severely that the doctors say he'll never walk again and you have a Glen Cunningham – who set the world's one-mile record in 1934. Deafen him and you have a Beethoven. Have him or her born black in a society filled with racial discrimination and you

have a Booker T. Washington, a Marian Anderson, a
George Washington Carver...

'Call him a slow learner, "retarded" and write him off
as uneducable and you have an Albert Einstein.' [11]

No excuses. No victims. No crybabies. No nonsense. No
paranoia!

The world is not plotting against us, but life is tough.
Problems and pain exist, but they must never be allowed
to conquer the soul.

The indomitable heart of the Super Achiever marches
on...

REFERENCES

1   Helen Keller, *Helen Keller's Journal*, 1938.

2   William Shakespeare, *Hamlet*.

3   Dylan Thomas, *Do Not Go Gentle Into That Good Night*.

4   Ebony, June, 1977.

5   Dr Chris Thurman, *The Truths We Must Believe*, Thomas Nelson Publishers, 1991.

6   *Old Testament Bible, Psalm 46:1, KJV*, Thomas Nelson Publishers, 1982.

7   Ravi Zacharias, *Can a Man Live Without God*, Word Publishing, 1994, p. 60.

8   Eugene Griessman, *The Achievement Factors*, New York, Dodd, Mead & Co., 1987, p. 81.

9   Ibid, p. 82.

10   Ibid, p. 90.

11   Ted Engstom, *The Pursuit of Excellence*, Grand Rapids Michigan, Zondervan, 1982, pp. 81–82.

CHAPTER 7
IN PRAISE OF TALL POPPIES
Abundance Mentality

'If you are 20 and not a socialist, you lack a heart. If you are 40 and not a capitalist, you lack a head.'

Winston Churchill

There are many on the ladder of success who believe that in order to get to the top they have to dislodge those above them and tread on those beneath them. Success, however, is not a ladder, it is a journey along a road on which we can all travel. The travellers upon this road, if they really want to get to the destination, are better off helping their fellow travellers, not attacking them.

Super Achievers do not operate with an 'I win, you lose' mentality, but with an 'I win, you win' idea of life. This is initially surprising for, when we begin to study the lives of those who qualify to be Super Achievers, it probably would be expected that we would find individuals who are highly competitive and fight to win at all costs. Interestingly, this type of attitude is a rarity.

Super Achievers understand that individual success does not necessarily mean the failure of others. They have what I term an *abundance mentality*. They want to succeed, they want to do well, they want to reach their goals and they are not in any way hampered by a feeling of guilt. Guilt only accompanies those who think in terms of 'I win, you lose'.

The scarcity mentality sees the economic world as a kind of pie with only so many pieces to go around. The more I get on my plate, the less for everyone else. If I consider this to be a good thing I become confrontational and competitive. If I consider this to be a bad thing I become demotivated and guilty of success. In an effort to appease conscience, I lower my standards and give in to the falseness of the tall poppy syndrome… I settle for mediocrity.

The truth is, life is not like a pie. The more I receive does not mean the less everyone else receives. Conrad Black, the Canadian media baron, puts it this way:

> *'It is the myth of the left and one of the wellsprings of the pervasive spirit of envy, that the success of a person implies the failure or exploitation of someone else. Our economic system is not based upon single combat war or a zero sum game.'* [1]

I cannot, as a believer in a good God, accept that the system for advancement he created has been designed with this inevitable, win-lose paradigm. The notion that one person's gain must be another's loss simply does not gel and is contradicted by the concepts of service, giving, team and family.

On the other hand, success does not just occur naturally and spontaneously. Paul Zane Pilzer elaborates on this point:

> *'… Our Father did not put us on this earth to profit at the expense of one another. Implicit within this belief is our understanding that, like a loving father, God would not simply hand over to us, his children, everything we desired. Rather, he would give us the*

*tools that we require to succeed, and allow us to
discover for ourselves how to use them.'* [2]

Life is more like a river. There is plenty for everyone. The
pie analogy only works, thinking of it in purely economic
terms, if we give to the pie the possibility of expansion.
Creativity, entrepreneurship and individual effort cause
such growth.

All our lives we have been subjected to an economic model
based on scarcity theory. That is, there is a limit to the
amount of available wealth. The traditional view has
forgotten the element of human ingenuity which
constantly redefines what has value and what does not.

Paul Zane Pilzer explains this in his historical overview
of valued resources. He points out that in the nineteenth
century the supply of whale blubber shrank, so we found
a way to make use of the worthless black goo that oozed
from the ground in Texas. Today, the most important
technology, the microchip, is made out of the most
common material – sand.[3]

Population may have increased but gross world product
continues to increase at a much higher and exponential
rate. Not only is progress continuing but the progress of
progress as well.

This simply means that the average worker's buying power,
per hour of work, is steadily increasing. The concept of

unlimited wealth is a point which has been vigorously debated in economic circles. It culminated in a bet between Julian Simon (author of *The Ultimate Resource* – a book which argues that people are that resource) and Paul Ehrlich, hero of the gloom and doom set.

In 1980 Simon issued the challenge to bet that the future price of any natural resource at any future date would be reduced. Ehrlich accepted and the bet was formalized in October 1980.

The combined prices of five metals – chrome, copper, nickel, tin and tungsten were chosen. Should the price rise Ehrlich would win. If it dropped, Simon would collect. Ten years later the bet was settled with Simon victorious. The price for the metals had fallen to 57.6 per cent of the 1980 price. If we include the effect of inflation, the price was as low as 30 per cent of the 1980 figure. [4]

Wealth is not limited to physical resource but to human creativity.

The nation of Singapore is a good example of this. Over the last forty years, without the necessary raw materials, physical space or rich arable farm land, this country has grown its economy considerably. They simply added to the picture: initiative, dreams, entrepreneurship, wisdom and persistence.

A person only has to talk to those brought up with a background of socialism, or one of its kindred philosophies, to understand that the dream of egalitarianism is never realized. When we continue to penalize those who achieve in life and subsidize those who refuse to take initiative, we are failing. Failing to understand that helping and rewarding the achiever causes resources, expertise and all their ancillary benefits to flow down to everybody in society.

Bureaucratic red tape that continually tries to level the playing field can often dissipate the very qualities that are necessary for the success of a society.

'When faith dies, so does enterprise. It is impossible to create a system of collective regulation and safety that does not finally deaden the moral sources of the willingness to face danger and fight, that does not dampen the spontaneous flow of gifts and experiments that extends the dimensions of the world and the circles of human sympathy.

'The ultimate strength and crucial weakness of both capitalism and democracy are their reliance on creativity and courage, leadership and morality, intuition and faith. But there is no alternative, except mediocrity and stagnation... Certain knowledge, to the extent it ever comes, is given us only after the moment of opportunity is passed. The venturer who awaits the emergence of a safe market, the tax cutter who demands

full assurance of new revenue, the leader who seeks a settled public opinion, all will always act too timidly and too late. [5]

Capitalism, when married to a strong moral framework and values base which includes philanthropy, duty and faith, should result in the rich and the poor getting richer. Surely the truth is that if the rich are not getting richer, they are doing something wrong. To be wise and proactive when one already has resources to work with, should create more wealth and as a result benefit rather than harm society. So then, Super Achievers realize that their success is also a way of helping other people.

While it may be true that the gap between rich and poor is growing, it should also be true that the poor are doing better as well. The best way to help a society is to encourage those with the money to use it, invest it, spend it and give it. This will create a growing economy, increased employment and more opportunities.

George Gilder, in his book *Wealth and Poverty*, produces a lengthy and compelling argument for what he calls *supply side economics*. He shows that there is nothing wrong with those who are well off shouldering more responsibility for the well-being of their society. This is often reflected in graduated tax rates. However, when the rate approaches or surpasses 50%, the revenue received by government actually begins to reduce. This is simply the result of those at this level beginning to work much harder at minimizing their tax. Add to this the dwindling incentive for earning more money, and one begins to see the practical truth of Gilder's position.

The Laffer curve reveals this theory in a simple way. Economist Arthur Laffer realized that there are probably two different tax rates that will produce a similar amount of revenue. For example, a zero rate will bring in no revenue, and a 100 per cent will also result in nothing because it would put a stop to taxable enterprise. Lower tax rates stimulate business and move capital into taxable activity, thus increasing revenue for government. Achievers again begin to achieve, cash flow throughout society is increased, employment rises and projects designed to help the needy and those dependent upon society are better resourced.

The Super Achiever is never threatened by someone else's success. They do not allow jealousy or greed to dominate their thinking processes. They understand the wisdom of Proverbs when it says *'The bountiful eye will be blessed'*. [6] We must realize that our own success should help others, and not hinder them. When this truth is understood we will begin to move out of the fog of self-interest and the destructive style of confrontational competition, into the clear light of freedom and achievement.

The tall poppy next door should inspire us to grow and provide us with shade. To cut it down is to join the throng of those who believe that mediocrity is normal and that colour, vibrancy and dreaming are somehow culpable for the ills of society. That grey, formless world shuns challenge and risk taking. It is no place for the Super Achiever to live.

The tall poppy next door should inspire us to grow and provide us with shade. To cut it down is to join the throng of those who believe that mediocrity is normal.

REFERENCES

1   Conrad Black, *A Life in Progress*, Random House, 1993.

2   Paul Zane Pilzer, *God Wants You to be Rich*, Zane Publishing Inc., 1995, p. 33.

3   Ibid, p. 33.

4   Tierney, *Betting the Planet*, as quoted by Pilzer, Ibid p. 55.

5   George Gilder, *Wealth and Poverty*, ICS Press, 1993, p. 37.

6   *Old Testament Bible, Proverbs 22:9, KJV*, Thomas Nelson Publishers, 1982.

CHAPTER 8
MY BRAIN HURTS
Constant Learning

'Anyone who stops learning is old, whether at 20 or 80. Anyone who keeps learning stays young.'

Henry Ford

The quest for knowledge, insight and wisdom is part and parcel of the life of the one who excels. The reason for this is self-evident. Super Achievers realize that as the circle of knowledge grows, so also does the boundary of ignorance. Or, to put it another way, the more we learn, the more we realize what we don't know. A revelation of how much we don't know will continue to motivate us towards learning.

There are many things in life I know. I know how to drive a car. I know how to speak English. I know how to make Bearnaise sauce (although the right application of that knowledge evades me more often than not!). Alternatively, there are many things I don't know. I don't know how to speak Chinese, I don't know how to navigate the Amazon, I don't know how to make an igloo. There are other things that not only do I know, but I know that I know them; things I have a certain and absolute knowledge of. I know that I know that my name is Phil Baker. I know that I know that I live in Australia.

Then there are many things that I don't know, but I know that I don't know them. I don't know how to be a handy man around the house. I don't know how to fix an automobile if it breaks down. However, I have an advantage over many other men in that, although I don't know these things, I know that I don't know them! Therefore I don't attempt to fix the car or to mend the broken gate, much to the relief of my wife! She is happy because when things are broken we get a suitably qualified person to come, and the broken items are fixed professionally. The few times I have tried to dabble in this area, disaster was almost always the result.

A little while ago in our house the lights blew a fuse. Being the gallant man of the family and having just watched an episode of *Home Improvement*, I declared to my wife and children, 'No problem. Father is here!' I went out to the fuse box and tried to remove the faulty fuse. I discovered it was jammed in its socket, so with a screwdriver I began to prise it loose – before a belt of electricity knocked me over. Concurrent with the surge of power there was a flash of insight that told me I had forgotten to turn the mains off! So you can see, I have an amazing capacity to make a mess of many home repair tasks, even changing a fuse. Thus you can understand the joy of my family when I declare that I know that I don't know about such matters.

Where is all this leading us? Well, if there are things that I know, and things that I don't know; things that I know that I know, and things that I know that I don't know – think how many things there must be that I don't know, and I don't know that I don't know them!

I am happily enjoying my life, doing what I am called to do and yet there is a multitude of things concerning what I do, that I don't know about, and I don't even know that I don't know them. This revelation alone will cause me to be a continual learner. Maybe today, in a seminar, reading a book, in a relationship, during a conversation,

I might learn something that I didn't know, which will enable me to be more effective in the journey that lies ahead.

Super Achievers, as a result, are always reading, listening to others and seeking advice. The book of Proverbs puts it this way: *'A wise person increases in learning, but a fool despises knowledge and instruction.'* [1] The biblical fool is not one whose IQ is deficient, but one whose attitude to life is that of non-absorption and the refusal to listen.

Art Buchwald, one of America's greatest humorists, has put it this way:

> *'There are too many people who think they're educated because they have a diploma. They aren't. You don't get educated; you prepare yourself for an education. You prepare yourself to know how to look things up, to know how to use books, how to think.'* [2]

The love of learning; the love of books is a common trait for Super Achievers. Truman was a constant reader, as was Kennedy. The latter's reading of history was a key to the decision-making process during the Cuban Missile Crisis.

Kennedy had been reading Barbara Tuchman's history of World War I, *The Guns of August*. He was amazed at how the beginning of the war could have been avoided. Over-reaction, prejudices, personality clashes... he was determined that the same mistakes would not be made in what could have become World War III.

The importance of input cannot be overstated. Our thinking has a direct connection to our actions. To change how we behave we must change how we think, and therefore solid nutritional brain food is essential.

As Griessman writes, *'High achievers may attain breadth of knowledge, but they always obtain depth of knowledge in some area. They may know a little about a lot of things, but they always know a lot about one thing.'* [3]

Mental breadth and depth are expanded as we take in sound information and give ourselves to purposeful contemplation. Blaise Pascal, my favourite philosopher, put it this way:

> *'Man's greatness lies in his power of thought.'*

The arrogance of youth, which refuses to ask questions, has destroyed many a life. Those that wish to get ahead must pursue those that have already got there and pick their brains for answers, ideas and perspectives on life. In this sense, one could rightly call the Super Achiever a humble person, in that they never think they know it all, and are always open to the advice and input of those around them.

Remaining objective is the key. Great learning must be accompanied by the willingness to listen to others. This is an important point and should not be glossed over. The tragedy of the intellectual is all too often the incipient and slow creeping arrogance that blinds the mind and limits the boundaries of growth. We can get too clever for our own good and, by looking for the intricate, miss the elegance and simplicity of truth.

G.K. Chesterton makes this point well:

> 'Now, one of these four or five paradoxes which should be taught to every infant prattling at his mother's knee is the following: that the more a man looks at a thing, the less he can see it, and the more a man learns a thing the less he knows it. The Fabian argument of the expert, that the man who is trained should be the man who is trusted would be absolutely unanswerable if it were really true that a man who studies a thing and practised it every day went on seeing more and more of its significance. But he does not. He goes on seeing less and less of its significance.'[4]

We must realize that to reach our goals we will need as much help as we can get. We should not confuse the getting of information with its application – with wisdom. The achiever asks penetrating questions that will yield practical results on the road to destiny. This continued reality-check, helicopting up to see the big picture, is a key practice that will keep us on track.

Input is Vital

The realization that input is vital for success, that right input leads to right results, carries with it a natural corollary. Wrong input will lead to wrong results. What we feed on, as individuals, will affect our thinking, then our beliefs and finally our actions. In this information age where the chatter in cyberspace can be deafening, it is important to screen what we allow into our hearts and minds.

Super Achievers realize that a constant diet of garbage, misinformation or negativity could derail them on the journey towards their life goal. The continual learning habit must be accompanied by selectively sifting through the available informational resources, in such a way as to ponder and study only those things that inspire, challenge and lead to growth and health. Unfortunately today, our society seems to have mistaken quantity of information for quality. Our press is filled with gossip rather than news, our churches can tell us what God won't do rather than what he will do. Our relationships can be draining rather than replenishing and our television is filled with what Chesterton called *'Chewing gum for the mind'*. Chewing gum is good in its own place but a constant diet of it will lead to malnourishment and loss of energy.

Rousseau once said that truth is to be sought not in the ideas and behaviour of corrupt dwellers of sophisticated cities but is more likely to be found in the pure heart of a simple peasant or innocent child. Our lives are surrounded by, and revolve around, trivia. There simply is no time and no example to point us elsewhere.

The sports scores interest us more than the sunsets. Our eyes are on the detail, the picture eludes us. Too busy watching *Friends* on television to be friends in life. We are like photographers on a wedding day: so intent on our task of capturing the moments, that to us the photo has become more real than the life it portrays. One wonders if tourists would see more and live more if they were not continually looking through the lens. Life is not a dress rehearsal. We must stop now and then to look and ponder.

In Praise of Thinking

> *'Most people think only once or twice in their lifetime. The reason I have been so successful is that I have been able to think once or twice a year.'*
> Victor Hugo

Our brains are amazing pieces of equipment, able to process 30 billion bits of information at once while utilizing the equivalent of 6000 miles of wiring and cabling. Yet this neural network can sit mostly dormant for a lifetime.

We must learn how to think. We must educate our children in a way that trains them to reason and discern, not just do.

The problem with outcome or vocational education theory is that it produces capable workers who are unable to operate successfully outside the narrow parameters of their job description.

Employers lament the lack of thinkers graduating from our major institutions. I am not talking here about IQ, but about the creative, imaginative breadth of knowledge-type people who are more than simply processors of information.

The push to remove art subjects; english, philosophy, history and the like from our curricula, is the chief culprit for this loss of enquiring minds. Sir Robert Jones, for many years New Zealand's leading real estate entrepreneur, is just one of the growing number of frustrated employers.

He tells of a recent management conference his company conducted for its top managerial trainees. The subject under discussion was techniques for leasing vacant space in a weak market. Jones pointed out to the trainees, that in more competitive foreign markets the practice was to put signs on buildings. This traditionally had not been done in New Zealand, as these spoiled the buildings' appearance and, until recently, it was relatively easy to lease space without taking such measures.

"Should we now adopt this practice?" I asked.

*'There followed a generally inane discussion, so I
narrowed the issue and put the proposition, "Why do
you suppose other nations continue doing this year
after year?" Someone pitifully suggested because it
might be considered good advertising for the real
estate company. The others sat in stupefying silence.
The obvious answer "because it works", was totally
beyond those heavily university-degreed minds.*

*'These people are not stupid… but they can't think.
They have gone straight from college and acquired
their law and commerce degrees and missed out on an
education. Sadly, what we are finding in our company
is that many of our best thinkers have never been near
a university…'* [5]

The fault is partly with the employers as well. It is easy in
this technical world to hire people based on grades and
diplomas without placing value on the benefits of a classical
education.

It has been humorously observed that a graduate with a
science degree asks, 'Why does it work?'. The graduate
with an engineering degree asks, 'How does it work?'.
The graduate with an accounting degree asks, 'How much
will it cost?'. The graduate with an arts degree asks, 'Do
you want fries with that?'!

Times, however, are changing. People are beginning to realize the importance of ideas and the power of the individual's thinking process.

It was Ed Cole who observed that the person without an organized system of thought is always at the mercy of the person who has one. Thus we must strive to develop this crucial area of our life, both in the continual getting of information and in the discipline of imaginative and creative thought.

The heart and mind of the Super Achiever requires jet fuel, not watered-down diesel, to reach the life goal. We must listen to big people and immerse ourselves in the big ideas of our world. There simply is not enough time for superficial, pedantic or banal things to dominate our cognitive abilities. We need inspiration, not just information. We need courage, not cowardice. We need passion, not pettiness. We will discover ourselves with solitude and searching, not superstitions and soap operas. We will finally reach our destination with discipline and deep thinking, not dalliance and diversion.

*Mental breadth and depth
are expanded as we take in
sound information and give
ourselves to purposeful
contemplation.*

REFERENCES

1   *Old Testament Bible, Proverbs 1:5, NIV,* New York International Bible Society, 1978. Used by permission of Zondervan Bible Publishers.

2   Eugene Griessman, *The Achievement Factors,* New York, Dodd, Mead & Co., 1987, p. 49.

3   Ibid, p. 25.

4   G.K. Chesterton, *The Twelve Men, Tremendous Trifles,* New York, Dodd, Mead & Co, 1910.

5   Robert Jones, *Punch Lines,* Inprint, 1991, p. 73.

CHAPTER 9
LIFESTYLES OF THE RICH & MISERABLE
Contentment

'I want to be what I was when I
wanted to be what I am now.'

Graffiti, London 1980

Out of all the qualities we have looked at, contentment seems to be the most elusive. The truth of *inside-out* is easily drowned out by the many voices of *more*.

To be honest, for our generation, there is more to have, much more. Jesus pointed out that real life does not consist in the abundance of possessions, yet surely this is not true for us... I mean, after all, now we have our central locking and our espresso machines, widescreen TVs and designer dogs. Magazines such as *The Robb Report* or *Gourmet Traveller* devote themselves to showing us what is available, and that we would be more fulfilled and contented if only we had... The only trouble is that, after the Lear jets and the limousines, the *if only* remains.

The more we have, the more we want. External wealth often produces internal craving, and so the cycle repeats itself.

The winter of our discontent progressively gets colder and drearier. It deadens joy, removes wonder and reduces life to just survival.

Constant craving for what is not, robs us of the ability to enjoy and celebrate what is. In the words of Shakespeare: *'striving to better, oft we mar what's well'*.

I used to be happy with flying. The excitement of the trip, the power surge of take-off, the movie, the audio channels, the view. Happy, that is, until I had the opportunity of flying first-class between Sydney and Los Angeles.

A friend had arranged a special ticket for almost the same price as a regular economy, so I jumped at my chance to experience life at the front of the plane. Upon check-in I began to notice the differences. I was called 'Mr Baker', and 'sir', instead of the normal 'Ticket please', and 'No, all the aisle seats have gone.' I was taken to a special lounge and enjoyed the Chardonnay and the Camembert. The airline then boarded. All those *other people* first, so that when we were asked to join the flight there were no queues or noise. Just classical music, French champagne and seats that actually were seats!

The personal video screen, complete with sports, documentaries and all the latest movies was my next discovery, but nothing could prepare me for dinner. Up to this point in time, the phrase *airline food* was an oxymoron, like *council worker* or *military intelligence*. How quickly that concept changed.

Beluga Caviar...

'Would you like Russian vodka with that sir?'

Fillet steak, medium rare with fresh asparagus.

'Béarnaise sauce, sir?'

Chocolate parfait, international cheeseboard with a choice of Chateau d'Yquem, vintage port or brewed coffee.

'Or would you like all three sir?'...

Later on during the flight, after my second movie, I decided to venture out of my stress-free environment. Call it nostalgia, call it gloating, but I was going to go through *the curtain*.

The first stage of my walk was through Business Class. Seats slightly smaller, occupants slightly more ambitious. I felt their grudging respect, as I was one of the few passengers that were better off than they. The second curtain loomed before me. British Airways call their Business Class, Club World. First Class is referred to as Fantasy World. I was, however, about to step into Third World. The scene that confronted me was all too familiar. People trying to sleep in positions they could not normally hold for more than a few minutes. Babies crying. Queues to the toilets. The obligatory rugby team calling for another round. I beat a hasty retreat to the safety and security of life at *the front*.

This whole experience has taught me several things. First of all, I am a first-class citizen. I belong there. I desire to be there. I need to be there! Secondly it taught me that the *upgrade* is worth both bribery and begging. (Free copies of this book are available to any airline personnel who have this coveted power of granting the *upgrade*!)

Thirdly, I have discovered that now I don't enjoy flying – no longer am I content in my economy seat. I know what lies beyond *the curtain*!

Contentment is the Holy Grail everybody seems to be searching for. Money, respect, pleasure and success are merely the chosen roads that the travellers hope reach this destination. Yet, as Ravi Zacharias points out, contentment remains elusive for many:

> *'One of the common refrains we hear from those who have reached the pinnacle of success is that of the emptiness that still stalks their lives, all their successes notwithstanding. That sort of confession is at least one reason the question of meaning is so central to life's pursuit. Although none like to admit it, what brings purpose in life for many, particularly in countries rich in enterprising opportunities, is a higher standard of living, even if it means being willing to die for it. Yet, judging by the remarks of some who have attained those higher standards, there is frequently an admission of disappointment…'* [1]

Zacharias then proceeds to give some examples:

> *'After his second Wimbledon victory, Boris Becker surprised the world by admitting his great struggle with suicide. Jack Higgins, the renowned author of "The Eagle has Landed" has said that the one thing he knows now, at this high point of his career, that*

he wished he had known as a small boy is this: "When
you get to the top, there's nothing there."[2]

To this could be added the words of Lee Iacocca, Chairman
of Chrysler:

'Here I am in the twilight years of my life, still
wondering what it's all about... I can tell you
this, fame and fortune is for the birds.'[3]

He goes on to explain that for him it was only family and
close friends that brought the contentment that he so
deeply desired.

John Gatto, New York's Teacher of the Year from
1989–1991, lamented the impact of materialistic thinking
on young people:

'Think of the things that are killing us as a nation.
Drugs, brainless competition, recreational sex, the
pornography of violence, gambling and alcohol. And
the worst pornography of all – life devoted to buying
things – accumulation as a philosophy. All are
addictions of dependent personalities...'

For many, contentment is tied up with what we have, and
how much we earn, yet study after study reveals that
satisfaction isn't so much getting what you want but
wanting what you have.

In other words, there are two ways to be rich. One is to have great wealth. The other is to have few wants. In his book, *The Pursuit of Happiness*, David Myers recounts how this truth was observed by a former nurse in a Nigerian village:

> 'A group of five to seven-year-old boys wearing rags for clothes were racing along our compound's driveway with a toy truck made of tin cans from my trash. They had spent the greater part of the morning engineering their toy – and were squealing with delight as they pushed it with a stick. My sons, with Tonka trucks parked under their beds, looked on with envy.'[4]

One has only to watch the family dynamic of children playing with their parents on a street in Calcutta. Compare this with the formal, restless and busy existence of most Western world, middle class homes, and we quickly realize that there is more to life than simply cash flow.

Making more money does not increase happiness. Being rich is something we have or don't have within us...

Thomas Ludwig together with David Myers, in studying the money–happiness question, revealed how we create our own discontent when we describe our inability to buy everything as poverty. Such *poor talk* (grumbling about the price of milk and bread on the way to and from the store in our new four-wheel-drive) is highly objectionable. We need to be more honest and admit that when spending outstrips income, the problem is lack of discipline or priorities, not that we are unable to afford life's necessities.

Such talk is not only offensive to those who are truly poor but also pollutes our thinking and magnifies our discontent. We begin to believe our own propaganda and reduce ourselves to self-pitying victims who are whingeing about what two thirds of the world's population would rejoice over. Thus we need to change our vocabulary, as Myers writes:

> "'I need that" can become "I want that." "I am underpaid" can become "I spend more than I make." And that most familiar middle class lament, "We can't afford it!" can become, more truthfully, "We choose to spend our money on other things." For usually we could afford it… if we made it our top priority; we just have other priorities on which we choose to spend our limited incomes.'[5]

So what is this secret art of contentment? I believe that as we all begin to practise the habits and cultivate the attitude of the Super Achiever, we will learn the truth of inward contentment. Such things as an overriding goal, focus, self-growth and humility are all prerequisites for internal harmony.

The lesson must be learned that contentment is not to be found necessarily in the palaces of the super-rich or around the boardroom tables of the business tycoons, but in the trusting, God-fearing and self-giving hearts of average people.

In looking back over my life I would have to say that when happiness and contentment levels were the highest, my external circumstances, house and income, were often at the lowest.

I can remember as a child, playing with my sister in a tiny back garden of a semi-detached house in a suburb of the Medway towns. We had hours of fun, playing with a tyre that swung from the only vegetation in the garden, a small, stunted and battered tree.

A year later, after emigrating from England to New Zealand, we found ourselves living on a small farm by a beautiful river mouth in the subtropical North. We had ocean beach and river front on our property. Fishing, surfing, canoeing or horse-riding were all available to us and yet it seems to me that life was more fun swinging from the tyre. *'The river of happiness is fed far less by wealth than by the streams of ordinary pleasures.'* [6]

In the final analysis, what we think is superior often disappoints. Discerning what is more, is easy; discerning what is better, is hard.

> *'What keeps our faith cheerful,'* says Garrison Keillor, *'is everywhere in daily life, a sign that faith rules through ordinary things: through cooking and*

small talk, through story telling, making love, fishing, tending animals and sweet corn and flowers, through sports, music, and books, raising kids – all the places where the gravy soaks in and grace shines through. Even in this time of elephantine vanity and greed, one never has to look far to see the camp fires of gentle and happy people.'[7]

REFERENCES

1   Ravi Zacharias, *Can a Man Live Without God?*, Word Publishing, 1994, p. 56.

2   Alister McGrath, *Intellectuals Don't Need God*, Zondervan, 1993, p. 15.

3   Lee Iacocca, *Talking Straight*, Bantam Books, 1989.

4   David Myers, *The Pursuit of Happiness*, Aquarian Press, 1993, p. 395.

5   Ibid, p. 45.

6   Ibid, p. 45.

7   Ibid, p. 45.

CHAPTER 10
FLYING WITH THE DUCKS
People Believers

'You've helped me become a more caring person McWhater, but now I don't need you anymore.'[1]

There is something about a great woman or man that radiates outward into the lives of those around them. This radiation is not just a natural occurrence but is the result of a purposeful belief in people. Super Achievers see the people around them from the perspective of their potential, rather than their behaviour. They are slow to carry a grudge and quick to forgive. They encourage, inspire and cause their friends, employees and co-labourers to grow larger on the inside. Very rarely do you find a Super Achiever who goes it alone.

More and more, great leaders of our day find the best way to work is to work through people, to build teams and to develop synergy.

This idea of synergy is an integral value in the life of Super Achievers. They honestly evaluate their own weaknesses and call others alongside who have abilities in those areas. They have an ability to draw on the strength of others and, as a result, become more effective and efficient in the journey towards their life goal.

To my mind, the concept of synergy has best been described, in the words of Zig Ziglar, as a group of ducks flying. If you have ever observed ducks in flight, you will notice immediately two things. First, they always fly in a V formation. Second, one side of the V is always slightly longer than the other side. The reason for both things is highly significant. First, the reason that one side of the

V is always slightly longer than the other side is simply that the side that is longer has more ducks in it!

On a more serious note, the reason ducks fly in a *V* formation is to take advantage of the partial wind vacuum created in the wake of each duck. By periodically changing the lead duck they can fly nearly twice as far together as they could on their own.

This truth of team is, I believe, self-evident. Not only is it the most effective way of getting things done but also the most fun. Marriages work best when couples work together.

Sports history is replete with examples of a team of average players defeating a group of gifted individuals.

A great music group is not so much about the brilliance of a solo act any of the musicians may bring to the table, but how well they play together.

Even in the dog-eat-dog world of business, this idea has resulted in a paradigm shift, as the number of business books released in recent years with the word *team* in the title can testify.

Super Achievers know that through tenacity, persistence, hard work, motivation, goal setting, vision and discipline, they will go a long way. However, if they can harness the energy, talents and dreams of the people around them, helping one another fulfil their destinies in life, then all in the team will excel, and the results are exponential. The Bible puts it this way: *'One will put a thousand to flight and two will put ten thousand.'* [2] One reason that many fail to achieve in life is simply because they find it very difficult to trust other people.

We judge on how we are. Trustworthy people are themselves trusting. Believing in others, to the point of naive optimism, often indicates sound character. The reason for their idealistic views about others is based on how they operate as individuals. This is why the one who is of doubtful character or criminal intent cannot trust other people to be honest. He knows himself too well and assumes that everyone is just like him.

A latent cynicism and mistrust in people will strike at the roots of significance every time. That is why the words of Jesus, about loving one another, are so important. We must refuse to allow the hurts, insults or injuries received, to dissolve our optimism and faith in humanity. To fail here is to limit our own hearts and therefore our life's progression. The glass ceiling of past hurt and bitterness is a primary reason for the loss of fulfilled destiny.

The willingness to be hurt enables us to experience the joy of relationships. Pain, coupled with the joy, is what life is all about.

This simple yet profound point has best been brought out in, of all things, a children's story about a much loved but battered toy:

'The Skin Horse had lived longer in the nursery than any of the others. He was so old that his brown coat was bald in patches and showed the seams underneath, and most of the hairs in his tail had been pulled out to string bead necklaces. He was wise, for he had seen a long succession of mechanical toys arrive to boast and swagger, and by-and-by break their mainsprings and pass away, and he knew that they were only toys, and would never turn into anything else. For nursery magic is very strange and wonderful, and only those playthings that are old and wise and experienced, like the Skin Horse, understand all about it.

'"What is REAL?" asked the Rabbit one day, when they were lying side by side near the nursery fender, before Nana came to tidy the room. "Does it mean having things that buzz inside you and a stick-out handle?"

'"Real isn't how you are made," said the Skin Horse. "It's a thing that happens to you. When a child loves you for a long, long time, not just to play with, but REALLY loves you, then you become real."

'"Does it hurt?" asked the Rabbit.

"Sometimes," said the Skin Horse, for he was always truthful. "When you are Real you don't mind being hurt."

"Does it happen all at once, like being wound up," he asked, "Or bit by bit?"

"It doesn't happen all at once," said the Skin Horse. "You become. It takes a long time. That's why it doesn't often happen to people who break easily, or have sharp edges, or who have to be carefully kept. Generally, by the time you are real, most of your hair has been loved off, and your eyes drop out and you get loose in the joints and very shabby. But these things don't matter at all, because once you are real you can't be ugly, except to people who don't understand."[3]

It is when we love and are loved, believe in others and sense their faith in us as well, that we discover what it is to become truly human. We cannot survive as simply autonomous units. This is the truth of community, of family and of friendship. We are part of one another. To disengage is to die. John Donne embedded this in our hearts and minds when he wrote:

'No man is an island, entire of itself; every man is a piece of the continent, a part of the main.'

To reach a goal on one's own is often a hollow and lonely experience. To bring a team, family or a group of friends together and see the dream realized corporately, brings community to success and success to community. In the final analysis, you see, we all need, in the words of Joe Cocker at Woodstock, *'a little help from our friends'*.

We must refuse to allow the hurts, insults or injuries received, to dissolve our optimism and faith in humanity. To fail here is to limit our own hearts and therefore our life's progression.

REFERENCES

1   'Cartoon', Across the Board, April, 1996, p. 15.

2   *Old Testament Bible, Deuteronomy 32:30, KJV.*

3   Margery William, *The Velveten Rabbit*, London, Heinemann, 1970, as quoted by Swindoll, *Improving Your Serve*, Hodder and Stoughton, 1991, p. 27.

CHAPTER 11
KEEPING OUT OF THE DITCHES
Balance

'Moderation is a fatal thing.

Nothing succeeds like excess.'

Oscar Wilde

Most of us like to think of ourselves as *well balanced*. The concept of balance, however, is highly subjective. One person's moderation is another's extreme. One person's floor is another person's ceiling. Yet I firmly believe that there is a middle of the road, and progress towards destiny is far more effective when our wheels are firmly on the asphalt rather than the verges.

Balance is, of course, not an equal amount of opposites. The half-good, half-evil person or the answer that is half-right and half-wrong, is not what we are talking about. Neither is the person who believes their relational equilibrium is in order simply because they have a chip on each shoulder.

Achieving balance is no mean feat, pardon the pun. We tend towards the edges; call it curiosity, call it adolescence, call it stupidity, but most of us, for most of the time, drive with a couple of wheels on the verge. We are this way individually, and we are this way as communities and nations.

Martin Luther, the Reformation leader, observed that the story of humanity was this way:

> '*History is like a drunken man, reeling from one wall to another, knocking himself senseless with every hit.*'

Dickens echoed this sentiment later: '*It was the best of times, it was the worst of times.*' [1]

Pascal highlighted this paradox as well:

> 'What a chimera then is a man! What a novelty! What
> a monster, what a chaos, what a contradiction, what a
> prodigy! Judge of all things, feeble earthworm, deposit
> of truth, a sink of uncertainty and error, the glory and
> the shame of the universe.'[2]

Why is it that we have this potential? Why could God not
have created humankind out of better stuff? C.S. Lewis
pointed out that the better the stuff something is made
of, the greater the potential for either extreme. A cow
can be neither good nor bad. A child, of course, can be.
An adult, either very good or evil. A genius, best or worst
of all.

Balance, then, whether we are talking about the individual
life or the whole nation, is a rare commodity. The question
is, does balance tend towards achievement, or is the
balanced individual one who is handicapped when it
comes to the race towards destiny?

When I first began to study this important area of reaching
goals and fulfilling dreams, I believed that extremists
would have the edge. Those who are prepared to sacrifice
everything on the altar of their passion stood a better
chance than those who were more balanced and whole.
I immediately thought of some people who have achieved
great things, people who were highly eccentric and totally
obsessed; people who have achieved greatness at the

expense of family, friends, their own health and life span. However, as I studied further, I began to realize that this supposition was way off the mark.

True success cannot be relegated to one division of life. A person who succeeds in business but fails in their personal relational world, and dies early of a work-induced heart attack, can hardly be called successful. Wholesomeness, health and success in every area of life are generally not found in those who are extreme. The Super Achiever is not found amongst the religious fanatics, food bingers, TV addicts or fasting martyrs. Success must be seen holistically; the result of maintaining priorities in life and keeping perspective. Those that excel in life often have a strong faith in God and belief in the family, with a sense of values, which causes them to live by conviction rather than preference.

This whole book is about the necessity of balance between inner and outer; that among our Lattes and laptops, our Machiatos and mobiles, we give thought to the soul.

Simple technological progress, despite its ability to make life more convenient, creates as many problems as it solves, as one writer alarmingly states:

'We did not know acid rain would result from burning fossil fuels. We did not know mobility would disrupt family and community stability. We did not know thalidomide would deform babies. We did not know

inner city housing projects would turn into ghetto war zones. We did not invent suburbs to throw our traffic patterns into chaos.' [3]

Progress has magnified our flaws and given us greater opportunity for self destruction. Richard Swenson makes this point well:

'We have put armaments in the hands of our hostility, litigation in the hands of our cynicism, affluence in the hands of our greed, the media in the hands of our decadence, advertisements in the hands of our discontent, pornography in the hands of our lust and education in the hands of our pride.' [4]

We are able to live faster but die quicker, if not on the outside, certainly on the inside. To use Solzenhitsyn's words:

'We are in an insane, ill-considered, furious dash into a blind alley.'

It is an interesting point to note, at this juncture, the fact that balance does not mean equal competence in all departments of life.

We all have strengths and weaknesses. There are some traits we excel in and others we spend our whole life working on simply to get to the point where they are not a hindrance. It would be wrong to assume that a Super

Achiever is one who has equal mastery over all the characteristics covered in this book. They may have a handle on the majority of them but no one is omni-competent.

Most prime ministers or presidents are voted in on their strengths and lose on their weaknesses.

Nixon was appointed because of his strong, directional, take-no-prisoners type of leadership, but departed on the blindspots that such a style often allows. That which we have nurtured in our life, the things we bring to the table, open doors. Our flaws and faults, if not realized and worked on, will quickly close them.

Balance then, is all about maximizing our strengths while working on our weaknesses so we do not become self-destructive.

The balanced life may not look, at first glance, as spectacular as that of the radical. Yet Super Achievers are more interested in significance than in showing off.

Life is a marathon not a sprint. There is no point in rushing to reach the top of the mountain and finally arriving at the summit so exhausted that one cannot enjoy the view, and having left the important people of our lives – family and friends – far below.

The error of externalism is often realized late in life and by then its consequences may have sabotaged many of the noble plans of youth. Oscar Wilde, who was quoted at the start of this chapter, was one who too late realized the benefits of balance. He spent the last years of his life in jail on a sodomy charge, and it was then that he probably penned these words:

> 'The gods have given me almost everything, but I let myself be lured into long spells of senseless and sensual ease. Tired of being on the heights, I deliberately went to the depths in search of a new sensation. What paradox was to me in the sphere of thought, perversity became to me in the sphere of passion. I grew careless of the lies of other people. I took pleasure where it pleased me, and passed on. And I forgot that every little action of the common day makes or unmakes character. And that therefore, what one has done in the secret chamber, one has some day to cry aloud from the house-top. I ceased to be lord over myself. I was no longer the captain of my soul, and I did not know it. I allowed pleasure to dominate me, and I ended in horrible disgrace.' [5]

Success must be seen holistically; the result of maintaining priorities in life and keeping perspective.

REFERENCES

1   Charles Dickens, *A Tale of Two Cities*.

2   Blaise Pascal, *Pensees*, Penguin Books, 1996.

3   Richard Swenson, *Margin*, Navpress, 1992, p. 31.

4   Ibid, p. 32.

5   Steve Farrar, *Finishing Strong*, Multnomah Books, 1995, p. 150.

CHAPTER 12
FIRST YOU HAVE TO GET OUT OF BED
Discipline

'The alternative to discipline

is disaster.'

Vance Havner

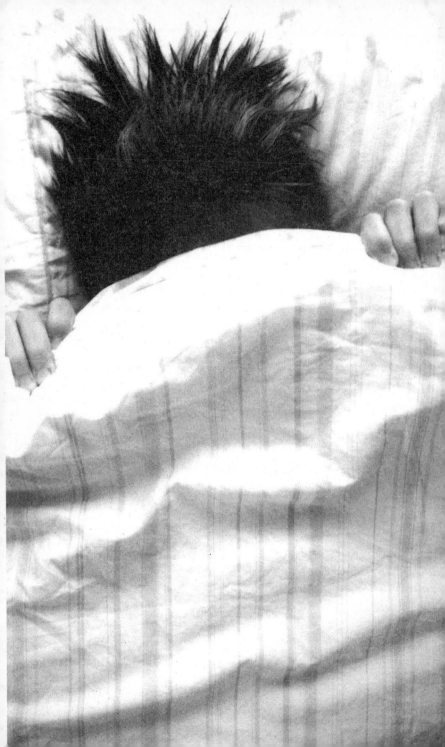

The best definition of discipline I have read was given by Scott Peck, who wrote, '*Discipline is the art of scheduling the pain and pleasure in life in such a way as to confront pain first so as to enhance pleasure later.*'[1] First there must be a realization that in life there is both pain and pleasure, and that it is impossible to avoid pain. Therefore, the disciplined individual will simply schedule in a way that deals with difficulties and problems quickly so that productivity and pleasure are enhanced.

The businesswoman who has ten things to do today, one of which is to phone an unhappy client, is disciplined if she makes that phone call first. She then feels better about herself and enjoys the rest of the day. However, if she defers the pain to the last thing on the agenda, the foreboding of the call weighs on her throughout the day, thus hindering her effectiveness.

The disciplined parent spends time with the children when they are young, thus building a relationship that will carry them through the possible trauma of teenage years. Disciplined sports people put time into practice and precision training, knowing that the pain of early mornings and repetitive exercises will be worth it when the games or competitions begin.

In a marriage relationship, if discipline dictates, problems are dealt with immediately.

The command, 'Do not let the sun go down on your wrath,' [2] if applied, would save many a couple. When bitterness, anger, resentment or offence are not dealt with in this way, they simply go underground and eventually poison the soil of the relationship.

As a husband, it takes discipline, guts and courage (some would even say stupidity!) to sit down and say to your wife, 'Honey, is there anything I do that annoys or frustrates you? I want you to talk with me about it…!'

This kind of question launches you into what psychologists would call the *tunnel of chaos*! Vulnerability is difficult, but not to deal with problems in marriage, in an open and honest way, simply delays the pain. Discipline realizes that the anguish of honestly dealing with problems now, is far less than the pain of separation and divorce later.

Discipline and Decisiveness

The ability to avoid the paralysis of inaction, and to defeat the fear of making mistakes is found in the discipline of decisiveness. It takes such discipline to realize that the pain of no decision in many areas of life is counter-productive.

Harry Truman, the United States President between 1945 and 1953, was well-known for such decisiveness. This was seen clearly in the decision to drop the atomic bomb on

Japan. Historians and political philosophers have argued long and hard, with the benefit of hindsight, over such decisions. Truman made them at the time with both courage and conviction.

Dean Rusk, former Secretary of State and close colleague with Truman during his career, spoke highly of this characteristic in the life of the leader:

> *'Harry Truman was a genius at making decisions. When he saw a complicated problem, with all the factors in it, it was as though he were looking at a heap of jumbled-up jackstraws. He would listen to all the briefing and think about it. Then he would decide which one of those jackstraws was the crucial one, from his point of view, and he would pull that one out of that complicated pile and make his decision, go home and go to sleep and never look back. He was a genius for that necessary oversimplification at the moment of decision. The alternative of that is paralysis.'* [3]

Converting the available information into action is what decision is all about. To know and not to do is not to know at all. The discipline of action, although it may give rise to mistakes, is far preferable to safe and stationary living. It was Lloyd Jones who said, *'The men who try to do something and fail are infinitely better than those who try to do nothing and succeed.'*

Developing Discipline

Discipline, I have discovered, has an intrinsic ability to be self-perpetuating.

The individual whose life is totally lacking in discipline need only concentrate on one area of his behaviour. It matters not what habit one chooses to reform – diet, exercise, sleeping schedule or punctuality. For when discipline begins in a corner of one's existence it will begin to grow, reproduce itself and breed. A sort of momentum takes over and our disorganized private world, much to our delight and surprise, is quietly conquered.

It is character's version of the domino theory. Yet the process must be started, and much energy expended in the first month in developing a discipline. Then energy and resolve are produced from this one area – enough to continue and more besides. On the other hand, once there is a break in the pattern, once we allow discouragement, laziness or even a simple holiday to erode these now well-cemented habits, momentum dies and entropy sets in. Chance again becomes our master and will invariably hand us the card: 'Go directly to jail, do not pass GO, do not collect £200.'

Anyone reading this book will be of the opinion that discipline is a prerequisite for achievement in life. Yet mere knowledge of one's need for a characteristic does not produce it. What then causes discipline to be developed and practised in the life of the Super Achiever?

Key to Discipline – A Sense of Destiny

We have already pointed out at the beginning of this book, that having an overriding goal or passion is the key ingredient to success. This is because once the goal and direction of one's life are set, they produce not only the motivation and the concentration, but the discipline necessary to pay the price for achieving the dream.

Having a vision of where you want to go will create incredible energy to do the hard things necessary to get there. The young man who continually refuses to clean his room, tidy his car, brush his hair, will often do these things without a hassle when, or if, the vision of a young lady fills his consciousness.

Vision will also give us strength to persist through the tragedies and injustices of life. The pain of jail, abuse and unpopularity are more easily tolerated and endured by those who have this sense of destiny.

Indeed, it is often the hard obstacles that test the mettle of our focus, challenge our sense of purpose and become the making or breaking of our lives.

The strength of our resolve and the power of discipline will come to the fore in testing times only if our internal direction is well calibrated and our life-purpose non-negotiable. Gandhi saw such times of persecution and imprisonment as necessary steps to fulfil his life quest.

Christ said that we must be willing to pick up our cross and follow him, implying that, in the fulfiling of major dreams, there is pain that must be confronted and lived through.

Without this willingness, without this discipline, we will not see the vision accomplished. The old weight-lifting maxim rings true here: *no pain, no gain.* A sense of destiny puts the power of discipline within our grasp.

Enjoy the Price

We have all heard the saying, 'You've got to pay the price for success,' and probably accepted its pragmatism without question. Life experience would declare, however, 'We don't really pay the price for success, we enjoy the price of success.' The first time I heard that expression was through the lips of Zig Ziglar. It hit me with real force. You see, we don't pay the price of a successful marriage, we enjoy the price of a successful marriage. We don't pay the price of being fit, we enjoy the price of being fit. We don't pay the price of being a good parent, we enjoy the price of being a good parent. We don't pay the price of being a Super Achiever, we enjoy the price of being a Super Achiever. We enjoy seeing our dreams accomplished and our goals reached, resulting in people being helped and our world becoming a better place.

Paradox of Freedom

'No man is free who is not master of himself.'
Epictetus

In today's world many do not understand the correlation between discipline and freedom. The truth is that the only really free person is the one who is disciplined.

The athletes who force themselves to train, to put in the long, hard hours, then have the freedom to perform to their potential. The musician who practises is the one who is also able to play from the heart with a freedom and spontaneity that the undisciplined can only watch and admire. The singer who is not willing to learn and practise is not free to sing in the way he or she desires. The young person who is undisciplined is never free to fulfil the dreams of the heart.

We are then most free when we are bound.

The Tragedy of Unfulfilled Potential

There is a price to success, but there is an even greater cost in settling for mediocrity and accepting the status quo. More potential has been lost to humanity through refusing to pay the price than any other cause.

The life of Samuel Taylor Coleridge has often been used as an example of how the promise of great talent can be short-circuited by the lack of discipline.

> 'Coleridge is the supreme tragedy of indiscipline. Never did so great a mind produce so little. He left Cambridge University to join the army; he left the army because he could not rub down a horse; he returned to Oxford and left without a degree. He began a paper called, "The Watchman" which lived for ten numbers and then died. It has been said of him: "He lost himself in visions of work to be done, that always remained to be done. Coleridge had every poetic gift but one – the gift of sustained and concentrated effort."
>
> 'In his hand and in his mind he had all kinds of books as he said himself, "completed save the transcription. I am on the eve," he says, "of sending to the press two octavo volumes." But the books were never composed outside Coleridge's mind, because he would not face the discipline of sitting down, to write out. No one ever reached any eminence, and no one having reached it, ever maintained it, without discipline.' [4]

The story of Coleridge could be repeated many times. The difference between the achiever and the Super Achiever often comes down to discipline.

The reason that most die with their music still in them is that they presume upon talent and expect their gifts to create success.

This philosophy of life gradually gives rise to a disappointment-driven melancholy, which will eventually permeate every moment of the day.

The loss of discipline will always signal the death of the dream. Enthusiasm and passion have their time. They belong to the race at its beginning and at its end when the applause of the crowd can be heard. Yet, for the bulk of the race, it is the steady steps, mile after mile, unseen and unappreciated, when discipline comes to the fore.

Without it, we have no hope. If our lives fail here it will cost us everything, but the price of discipline is paid with joy by those on the road towards destiny. These are they who see and understand. The tortoise of such character will always defeat the hare of superficial passion.

REFERENCES

1   M. Scott Peck, *The Road Less Travelled*, Arrow Books, 1990, p. 18.

2   *New Testament Bible*, Ephesians 4:26, NIV, New York International Bible Society, 1978. Zondervan Bible Publishers.

3   Eugene Griessman, *The Achievement Factors*, New York, Dodd, Mead & Co., 1987, p. 209.

4   William Barclay, *The Gospel of Matthew*, Westminster, p. 280, as quoted by Gordon MacDonald, *Ordering your Private World*, Highland Books, 1984, p. 70.

CHAPTER 13
I'M BIGGER ON THE INSIDE
Self-Growth

'Our grand business is not to see what lies dimly at a distance, but to do what lies clearly at hand.'

Thomas Carlyle

I have emphasised that success in life is inside-out. Many, however, make the mistake of going to work on that which is at a distance, rather than turning their attention to that which is close by.

We are not always able to change externals, but internal and life change can be accomplished when we begin to understand this task of personal growth.

The Super Achiever is committed to learn and grow in every area of life; to continually push the boundaries, not only in understanding, knowledge and wisdom, but in character, attitudes and endurance. This is frequently seen in its most basic level of keeping the body fit, eating right and exercising so that energy for the day is never a problem. Constant improvement and maintenance of health are outward reflections of this inner value. We must, however, go deeper yet, to realize that self-growth is a belief that must pervade and so affect our whole being.

Achievers in life are big people, or to use Aristotle's phrase, *'great souled'.*

Big people are not simply created by life, genetics or parental modelling. There has to be the willingness to push the boundaries of one's life, attitude and heart outward; to move out of the personal comfort zone of non-growth and lead the chase for personal change. It is madness to keep doing the same thing over and over again, expecting different results. We must understand, therefore, that the willingness to think, believe and act differently is the key to real, visible transformation.

Super Achievers are continually working on their character, emotional responses and spiritual life. They realize that success is inside-out, that the heart or the inner core of the person is where the hardest work must be done: that to grow on the outside, you must grow on the inside.

When, on the other hand, this order is reversed, when there is a sudden expansion of one's external world without a corresponding growth in the internal life, destruction is almost inevitable. The well documented despair of many who win major prizes through the lotteries is a good example of this truth. More money might be in the bank but often the relational and private worlds are devastated. The internal strength available is inadequate to carry and assimilate such an increase in external growth.

For several years I was involved in teaching children in a regular programme at our local church. I tried to make children's church, as we called it, exciting and dynamic and would often conduct various chemical experiments creating explosions and flashes of light. One experiment involved the placing of a small quantity of water in the bottom of a square gasoline can and heating the can until steam was coming out of the top. We would then quickly remove the can from the heat, put the lid on tightly and watch what would happen. Very slowly the can would begin to crumple until it was squashed and buckled. This happens because a partial vacuum has been created within the can and, as it begins to cool, the external air pressure eventually crushes the can. The pressure within is far less than that which is without.

So it is with life. The Super Achiever realizes that personal implosion is a very real possibility unless constant work is carried out on the heart. There are many ways of doing this. Benjamin Franklin practised what he called the 13-week programme. He wrote down 13 virtues that he wanted to maintain or practise in his life. Things such as humility, perseverance, forgiveness, friendliness and discipline. He would then assign one of these to each week and throughout that week concentrate on that one virtue; thinking about it and asking questions that brought both analysis and improvement. In this way, by working through the 13 weeks, he was able to devote at least four weeks of concentrated self-improvement on each of these virtues per year. Later in life he declared that this practice was probably the key habit of his life that enabled him to achieve everything he did. In simple terms, he was simply committing himself, through the use of a practical strategy, to self-growth.

A great benefit of faith in God is that you are continually compelled to be authentic and honest in the evaluation of weaknesses and faults. Such faith encourages repentance and promises forgiveness. Thus the individual is continually motivated to improve without falling into the ditches of a guilt-obsessed, work-based living on the one side, or of false pride and personal complacency on the other.

A personal and practical programme of self-growth will not only develop our capabilities in dealing with what life presents to us, but also enhance our ability to enjoy it.We will find we have energy left at the end of the day, and creativity and ideas left at the end of the problems. If you think about it, it is the only decent way to live.

One author calls this *margin*. Without the decision to grow on the inside we quickly surrender to the continual frustration of marginless living:

> '*Marginless is being thirty minutes late to the doctor's office because you were twenty minutes late to getting out of the hairdresser's because you were ten minutes late dropping the children off at school because the car ran out of gas two blocks from the gas station — and you forgot your purse.*
>
> '*Margin on the other hand is having breath left at the top of the staircase, money left at the end of the month, and sanity left at the end of adolescence.*' [1]

Many make the mistake of going to work on that which is at a distance, rather than turning their attention to that which is close by.

REFERENCES

1   Richard Swenson, *Living Above the Level of Mediocrity*, Word, 1987, p. 13.

CHAPTER 14
THE UPSIDE OF DOWN
Humility

'The devil did grin for his darling sin is pride that apes humility.'

Samuel Taylor Coleridge

John Cleese, best known for managing a small hotel in Torquay, has also done more serious work. He was the voice of Screwtape in the audio version of C.S. Lewis's classic book, *The Screwtape Letters*.

Screwtape, a senior devil, writes a series of letters to Wormwood, an apprentice demon, giving advice on how to destroy people's faith. His advice on using humility as a weapon is instructive:

> *'Your patient has become humble; have you drawn his attention to this fact? All virtues are less formidable to us once the man is aware that he has them, but this is especially true of humility. Catch him when he is really poor in spirit and smuggle into his mind the gratifying reflection, "By jove! I'm being humble," and almost immediately, pride at his own humility – will appear.'*

If only Basil Fawlty was as perceptive!

The story is told of the shipping magnate, Mr Onassis, who at the height of his power would conduct board meetings on his luxury yacht. Adjoining his office was a private bathroom and toilet that had been fitted with a two-way mirror on the door, thus enabling Mr Onassis to take a break from his meeting and yet be able to observe what the participants were doing and saying in his absence.

Mr Onassis was hosting a business meeting after the ship had been through a major refit. When he felt the call of nature and excused himself, he sat down on the toilet and looked up expecting to see the meeting continuing. Instead all he was looking at was a reflection of himself. A workman, making minor repairs to the door earlier in the day, had replaced the mirror the wrong way around!

We laugh at such stories for several reasons. First, all of us can identify with such experiences. We can all muster a list of personal, most embarrassing moments that, despite our attempts to fool the world that we have got it all together, show us up to be what we know we really are – total klutzes. Secondly, we enjoy hearing about others' mistakes, especially if they hold a position of prominence or are well-known. Deep down we suspect that the greats of our world haven't got it together either, and love the stories that bring out their human side.

We live in a world, however, where having it all together is portrayed as a prerequisite for success. Image is everything so we are rarely honest about our own inadequacies. Ours is a world of individualism and self-absorption. We have been desensitized to arrogance by the constant call to self-esteem; to believe in ourselves, and the 'I'm OK, you're OK' view of humanity. Add to this the basic misunderstanding of what humility really is, and we have the recipe for a world where pride is only thought of in positive terms; a world that also wonders why the sense of serenity and fulfilment does not follow its self-aggrandizement and selfish pursuits.

We need to renew our quest for humility. We need to take this character quality off the scrap heap where it has been wrongly defined and disposed of. We must take a fresh look at what humility actually is and look afresh at the tremendous benefits it brings to those who decide to develop it.

Mohammed Ali, for many, especially in his early years, was arrogance personified.

There is a story told, maybe apocryphal, of Ali flying to one of his engagements:

> 'The aircraft ran into inclement weather and was soon being tossed about by the moderate turbulence. The passengers were instructed to fasten their seat belts immediately. Everyone complied but Ali. Noticing this, the flight attendant approached him and requested he follow the captain's order.
>
> 'Ali simply responded, "Superman don't need no seatbelt." The flight attendant, not missing a beat, replied, "Superman don't need no airplane either."'[1]

What Humility is Not

Although we often talk about humble circumstances, humility is not based upon externals. Circumstances do not have the ability to make a person humble. There are both humble millionaires and proud prisoners. Sadly, those in the greatest need often tend to be the proudest of all. Humility is a condition of the heart, unrelated to position, wealth or achievement.

Others would define humility as a somewhat pathetic, self-reproving condition, the opposite to self-confidence and a bedfellow of self-pity. The doormat approach to life is an open invitation to those who abuse, use and manipulate. Such an attitude in life will do nothing to build self-respect or mature relationships.

We may desire to call this humility, but to do so is to malign a God-given quality. Humility increases the individual's effectiveness and serenity while this impostor, this wolf in sheep's clothing, this cowardly self-deprecation, never develops – only destroys.

Humility has received much bad press due to these pale imitators.

We must come to realize that true humility is always a sign of inner strength and never a symptom of weakness or self-doubt.

Humility Defined

Humility is the internal quality that prefers others and exalts them, while appraising one's self realistically. It is not so much a putting of one's self down, but the lifting up of others.

Humility realizes that the only decent way to live is to be motivated beyond yourself; to serve and help others, to be more interested in the giving than the getting. When this principle becomes an inner value and is practised with consistency, the getting will take care of itself. Zig Ziglar has put it this way:

> *'I can get everything I want in life by just helping enough other people get what they want.'*

Why Be Humble?

NUMBER ONE – THE MYSTERIES OF LIFE

The story is told of how President Roosevelt and a friend, naturalist William Belbe, would often go outside after dining together and look up at the stars. They would first look for a patch of light in the night sky near Pegasus, and then they would both say together the following few sentences:

> *'That is the spiral galaxy Andromeda. It is as big as our Milky Way and is one of a hundred million galaxies. It consists of a hundred billion stars each brighter than our Sun.'*

They would turn to one another and say, 'Feeling small enough now?' and then retire for the evening.

I personally believe that the latest scientific discoveries from the world of quantum mechanics and astrophysics heighten this awareness. It seems the more we learn about the origin of the universe and the processes of life, the more we are amazed.

The entire cosmos, it seems, is balancing on a series of razor blades... finely tuned characteristics each necessary for life to be possible. This phenomenon is known as the *anthropic principle*. As the months go by and our knowledge increases, so this principle rapidly becomes more and more impressive.

Cosmologist Edward Harrison states:

> *'Here is the cosmological proof of the existence of God –*
> *the design law of Paley – updated and refurbished.*
> *The fine tuning of the universe provides prima facie*
> *evidence of deistic design. Take your choice: blind*
> *chance that requires multitudes of universes or design*
> *that requires only one... Many scientists, when they*
> *admit their views, incline towards the teleological or*
> *design argument.'* [2]

Hugh Ross in his book, *The Creator and the Cosmos*, lists 25 such characteristics for the universe and a further 32 for our planet. The razorblade analogy is, if anything, too generous. Take, for example, one parameter that has to do with the electromagnetic force relative to gravity. If this was increased by one part in 10^{40} (that's 10 with 40 noughts after it!) only small stars would form. If it was decreased by just one part in 10^{40}, only large stars would form.

For life to be possible in the universe both large and small stars must exist. The former produce life's essential elements and the latter are the only stars that are stable enough and burn long enough to sustain a planet with life.

The narrowness of this parameter cannot be overemphasized. Ross gives the example of marking a five cent piece with a red cross and then throwing it into a pile of unmarked five cent pieces. A pile so large it covers the whole of Australia up to the height of the moon. Now multiply this pile by one trillion. 10^{40} is then the chance that a blindfolded man would have in picking the red five cent piece on his first attempt! [3]

Remember this is just one of the razor blades.

Tony Rothman, a theoretical physicist, in an essay on this *anthropic principle* said:

> 'When confronted with the order and beauty of the
> universe and the strange coincidences of nature, it's
> very tempting to take a leap of faith from science into
> religion. I am sure many physicists want to. I only
> wish they would admit it.' [4]

More and more are admitting it. Robert Griffiths, who won the Heinemann prize in Mathematical Physics, observed: *'If we need an atheist for a debate, we go to the philosophy department. The physics department isn't much use.'*

This, then, is why humility is enhanced the more we grow and the more we learn.

We will continue to learn, to explore, to stretch beyond ourselves. This is one attribute that makes us truly human – the search for truth. The more we discover of the puzzle, the more impressed we are with its manufacturer.

I heard of one individual who was obsessed with space exploration and the desire to prove a pet theory – that there was an identical, mirror planet of the earth on the other side of the sun. A planet that was as impossible to detect as we were to them.

When NASA refused to buy into the theory and dismissed the man as a crackpot, he set out to go it alone. Several years were spent in designing and building a simple one-man rocket for the express purpose of going to the other side of the sun.

Eventually this project was completed and our hero launched successfully and set off, only to collide halfway there with an identical rocket coming from the opposite direction!

This fascination of space and the desire to learn is also accompanied by something far deeper.

There comes a time, I believe, in the existence of every human being when we suddenly realize the enormity and wonder of creation and the seeming insignificance of our own life. Couple this with the inner awareness of a creator being, a creator who deems us highly significant, indeed the crowning accomplishment of his creation, and we are filled with a real sense of humble reverence and awe. Is not this the reason for the teaching and practice of worship, as found in religious faith – many would argue, one of its greatest strengths?

Worship enables us to maintain a healthy perspective on who we are and who God is. The fanciful doctrines of the new age movement, in which all of us are actually gods ourselves, know nothing of this. Pantheism offers a short term sense of being in control, where self is worshipped, but in the final analysis it fails to perform as the god of all feeling and meaning. To practise the worship of God in our existence, thinking and action is a major key in allowing the characteristic of humility to develop within us.

NUMBER TWO – THE DARK SIDE

'Out of the Crooked Timber of Humanity, no straight thing was ever made.' [5]

Humility recognizes that all of us are created and engineered for success and achievement, and yet, at the same time, knows that within us all there is a dark side. The 'I'm OK, you're OK' philosophy of life is only partly true. The blame mentality has exacerbated this false sense of our own uprightness.

This refusal to take personal responsibility, the redefining of sin as sickness, the reduction of punishment to just rehabilitation, have all contributed to our sense of cosmic smugness.

It seems we are incapable of being totally pure or right in our thoughts, motives and actions. Without calling on divine help, we are incapable of rising above the miserableness of the human condition.

This dark side is not just exhibited in the evil despots who have come and gone, but also in the phenomena of group-evil, when normal men and women stand by and allow that which is wrong to prevail, especially if to speak out is to cause personal harm or loss of popularity. Deep down we all know that if the secrets of our heart were laid bare, we would not be proud of our record.

The Times once produced an article entitled 'What's Wrong with the World?'. G.K. Chesterton, the writer, replied, *'I am. Yours truly, G.K. Chesterton.'*

Pride is often the result of overvaluing one's own talents or undervaluing those of others. Humility, however, is not into comparisons. Although I may have certain strengths, abilities or skills that others may not have, I also have weaknesses, flaws and faults that others may not share. In short, if my humility or for that matter my pride is based upon what I can or cannot do, I am deluded.

True humility recognizes that we are all wired up differently. We all have, in the words of the New Testament, different gifts. We maintain our balance and perspective when we think of ourselves in this light. We all have, as it were, something we can offer and bring to the table.

It is our obligation to use what we have been given for the common good. Humble people understand this and use their gifts confidently. When praise comes, they do not take the adulation to heart but thank their creator for making them so.

REFERENCES

1   As told by Ravi Zacharias, *Can a Man Live Without God?*, Word Publishing, 1994, p. 7.

2   Hugh Ross, *The Creator and the Cosmos*, Navpress, 1993, p. 111.

3   Ibid, p. 116.

4   Tony Rothman, *'Discovery Magazine'*, *What You See is What You Beget*, Theory, May, 1987.

5   Immanuel Kant, as quoted by Isaiah Berlin, *The Crooked Timber of Humanity*, John Murray Publishers, 1990, Preface.

CHAPTER 15
FORTUNE FAVOURS THE BRAVE
Courage

'All our dreams can come true
– if we have the courage to
pursue them.'

Walt Disney

There is something about courage that is incredibly inspiring. Whether one sees it in real life or reads about it in history, courage never fails to grab the heart and motivate the soul.

Hollywood has been quick to recognize this and therefore it tends to be the only secret of a Super Achiever we find regularly on our screens. Courage is portrayed as Rocky Balboa takes on a superior opponent or Arnold Schwarzenegger faces an all-powerful class of kindergarten children. Butch Cassidy and the Sundance Kid had it and so did the Karate Kid. Call me a barbarian, call me culturally impaired, but I actually enjoyed these films. I may not get an invitation to Cannes with such an admission, but there is something about raw courage and primitive man against the elements which gets the testosterone flowing.

Courage, of course, knows no gender boundaries. It is just that most men only recognize and appreciate it when it is conveyed in digital sound, widescreen, macho-type films. Yet deep down, most of us guys realize that if a Bond or a Rambo had to contemplate the experience of childbirth, their carefully crafted façades would crumble at the first contraction!

Courage comes in many different forms, but when it comes to us we must grab it, because success in life desperately needs its strength.

One cannot read a book like *Reach for the Sky*, view a film such as *Schindler's List*, or listen to a wartime speech by Churchill, without sensing the courage rising. With courage we can face the future with confidence. Courage enables us to endure our present problems with a tenacity that never gives in. Courage makes us stronger, braver and better people.

Webster's Dictionary defines courage as *'Quality of mind or spirit that enables one to face difficulty, danger and pain with firmness and resolve'*.

Courage is not the absence of fear, it is the ability to face fear and say, 'Regardless of how I feel at the moment, I am going to push through to the other side.'

Courage realizes that fear, more often than not, is illogical. Allowing fear to dominate makes the problem worse. Michel De Montaigne said, *'He who fears he will suffer, already suffers because of his fear.'*

Churchill, whose life epitomized this virtue, had this to say:

> *'One ought never to turn one's back on a threatened danger and try to run away from it. If you do that you will double the danger. But, if you meet it promptly and without flinching you reduce the danger by half. Never run away from anything!'*

Those who achieve realize that life involves some element of risk. One cannot cover every base. Success is never guaranteed. Ineffectiveness comes on the wings of fear. When the '*what if?*'s loom larger in our consciousness than the '*why not?*'s, then cowardice rules over courage and dreams go unfulfilled.

Pioneering always takes courage. As the Spanish poet Antonio Machado put it: '*Traveller, there is no path. Paths are made by walking.*' Courage ventures from the path and leads the way. It dares to be different and, as a result, expands the circle of human experience.

The bears, lions and Goliaths of life will never retreat of their own accord. They must be faced.

Fear says run. Courage stops and fights.

Our culture must fight for what is right and good; something that becomes impossible when the will has gone or the nerve to stand up for truth has faltered.

The life experiences of Solzhenitsyn caused him to write and warn of bravery's demise:

> '*Must one point out that from ancient times, a decline in courage has been considered the beginning of the end.*'[1]

Gandhi's courage was seen in his willingness to stand against oppression, and to stand up for truth regardless of personal consequence. His quiet persistence in imprisonment and fasting was maintained by the stamina that courage brings: Daniel facing the lions, Churchill facing the Nazis, Lincoln facing his self-doubt, Joan of Arc the fire. All who achieve rely heavily on this virtue.

Courage has been the key to many of the world's Super Achievers.

Jack Lemmon has said he tries to harness his fears and use them to work for him:

> *'I think we worry about failure too much. I don't think that failure very often can hurt anybody. It's fear of failure that will absolutely destroy you.'*

Others showed their courage, like Mary Kay, by investing all her retirement money into the new, yet risky business. Kris Kristofferson left his secure career in the army to pursue the untested and unknown future of the songwriter. When asked what qualities had helped him the most, he replied: *'A creative imagination and a compassion for my fellows and strength of spirit, which doesn't come from me but from God. I think I have a strong spirit. I allow my spirit to be strong.'*[2]

Courage itself very rarely stands alone. It is the by-product of faith and it is the child of destiny. This is, of course, one of the greatest discoveries of the Super Achiever: that a characteristic such as purpose, once cultivated, produces naturally the necessary ingredients to fulfil itself.

This is true of most virtues. With humour comes perspective and with perspective, peace. Focus produces both clarity and energy, whilst humility enables us to believe in others and continue to grow in knowledge and wisdom. When the decision is made, and the journey is embarked upon with conviction, the soul finds much help along the way.

Conversely, negative habits, attitudes and deficient character traits compound, working against the individual and their success: pride results in a loss of information and relationships; unforgiveness destroys our perspective of life and causes us to lose focus; hope and humour are not nurtured when we allow despondency or apathy to dog our path and paralyse our progress.

The domino effect will work either to our advantage or disadvantage. The heart, as it were, looks after those who look after it. The old dictum rings true – *God helps those who help themselves!*

The neglect of our inner world will slowly suck meaning out of our existence. Like quicksand, the melancholy of emptiness will finally have its inevitable victory.

Perhaps this is why the imperative of Proverbs must be heeded:

> *'Guard your heart above everything else you guard, for from it flow the very forces of life.'*[3]

When the *the* 'what if?'s *loom larger in our consciousness than the* 'why not?'s, *then cowardice rules over courage and dreams go unfulfilled.*

REFERENCES

1   Alexander Solzhenitsyn, *East and West*, New York, Harper and Collins, 1974, p. 745.

2   As quoted by Eugene Griessman, *The Achievement Factors*, New York, Dodd, Mead & Co., 1987, p. 216.

3   *Old Testament Bible, Proverbs 4:23, NIV*, New York International Bible Society, 1978. Zondervan Bible Publishers.

EPILOGUE
FURTHER ON, FURTHER IN

Our journey together has discovered and explored some qualities I believe are essential for success in life.

Obviously this particular study on the secrets of Super Achievers is not exhaustive and yet its lessons are compelling:

That the health of our souls, inside-out living, and ordering and expanding the inner world are the keys to finding ourselves and reaching our potential.

That the problem and the answer both lie within our hearts and therefore within our reach.

That the journey outward is not nearly as important or fruitful as the journey inward, and the forces of the soul must be nurtured if we are going to be the people we dream of.

It seems strange, does it not, that despite these truths, which I believe are self-evident and resonate within us all, our society and our culture continue in the worship of dead and impotent gods – selfishness and escapism, non-responsibility and accumulation… We are born for better things than these. Deep down we know the truth, but for some reason we don't live it out.

'*Whatever will be, will be*' is wrong!

Great lives don't just happen, they are caused!

Caused through desire, decision, determination and faith.

Caused by those who get desperate enough to buck the system and say 'No' to the security of mediocrity.

Caused by those who rouse themselves from the slumber of complacency and self-depreciation.

There is, you see, a strange malady sweeping our land. One akin to sleeping sickness or chronic fatigue syndrome. This ailment does not, however, strike the body, but the heart. Truth, which generations before us have felt no hesitation in dying for, draws only a slight smile and nod of passive agreement from us. The passion has been absorbed by the pleasure, the fire has gone out of our faith. The stakes are still sky-high, but for us it doesn't seem to matter any more.

Our life is, however, not some kind of Hollywood blockbuster, where danger threatens us as we watch, munching our popcorn, and knowing it's all just pretend. The forces arrayed against us are real. Eternity flows ahead of us… if we sleep now we do so at our own peril.

Let us take courage. Stand and fight. Let us be who we are meant to be. Life is for living. The years are passing. The time for decision is now!

*Great lives don't just
happen, they are caused!*

AUTHOR

Phil Baker is the best-selling author of several books including *Secrets Of Super Achievers* and *Wisdom – The Forgotten Factor Of Success*.

He is also a renowned international speaker, speaking to business people and at conferences and churches with audiences ranging from 50 to 10,000 people.

Phil lives in Perth, Australia, where he is the Senior Minister of Riverview Church, one of Australia's largest churches.

PHIL BAKER'S ONLINE DIARY
Visit Phil Baker's online diary where he regularly posts his thoughts and observations on a range of topics from politics, history, philosophy, theology, poetry, running and more stuff!

You can visit his BLOG at www.philbaker.net

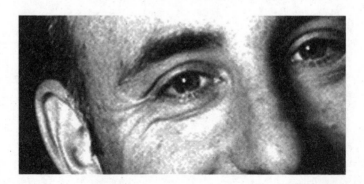

BIBLIOGRAPHY

Aikman, David.
Hope, the Heart's Great Quest, Servant Publications, 1995.

Anderson, Leith.
Winning the Values War, Bethany House Publishers, 1994.

Barrett, William.
Death of the Soul, Anchor Books, 1986.

Bell, Jones S. & Campbell, Stan.
A Return to Virtue, Northfield Publishing, 1995.

Bellah, Madsen, Sullivan, Swidler & Tipton.
Habits of the Heart, University of California Press, 1986.

Bennett, William J. (ed)
The Book of Virtues, Bookman Press, 1993.

Berlin, Isaiah.
The Crooked Timber of Humanity, John Murray Publishers, 1990.

Black, Conrad.
A Life in Progress, Random House, 1993.

Bode, Richard.
First You Have to Row a Little Boat, Harper Collins, 1997.

Buford, Bob.
Halftime, Zondervan, 1994.

Carnegie, Dale.
How to Stop Worrying and Start Living, Cedar, 1953.

Farrar, Steve.
Finishing Strong, Multnomah Books, 1995.

Frankl, Victor.
Man's Search for Meaning, London, Hodder and Stoughton, 1964.

Fraser, Antonia.
Cromwell, Our Chief of Man, Methuen, 1973.

Galbraith, John Kenneth.
The Culture of Contentment, Sinclair-Stevenson, 1992.

Gandhi, M.K.
An Autobiography, Penguin, 1982.

Gardiner, Howard.
Leading Minds, Basic Books, 1995.

Gilbert, Martin.
Winston S. Churchill, London, Heinemann, 1983.

Gilder, George.
Wealth and Poverty, ICS Press, 1993.

Griessman, B. Eugene.
The Achievement Factors, New York, Dodd, Mead & Co., 1987.

Hybels, Bill.
Honest to God, Zondervan, 1990.

Jahanbegloo, Ramin.
Conversations with Isaiah Berlin, London, Orion, 1993.

Jones, Barry.
The Macmillan Dictionary of Biography, Macmillan Press, 1986.

Jones, Bob.
Punchlines, Inprint, New Zealand, 1991.

Kawasaki, Guy.
Hindsights, Warner Books, 1993.

King, Martin Luther.
Strength to Love, Harper Collins, 1969.

Lash, Joseph P.
Helen and Teacher, The Story of Helen Keller and Anne Sullivan Macy, New York, Delacorte Press, 1980.

Lewis, C.S.
The Screwtape Letters, Fontana, 1953.

MacDonald, Gordon.
Ordering Your Private World, Highland Books, 1984.

Maxwell, John.
Developing the Leader Within You, Word, 1993.
Be All You Can Be, Victor Books, 1994.
Leadership 101, Honour Books, 1994.

Moir, Phyllis.
I Was Winston Churchill's Secretary, Hamstead Press, 1941.

Morris, Thomas.
Making Sense of It All, William B. Eerdmans Publishing, 1992.

Muggeridge, Malcolm.
Chronicles of Wasted Time, Vols. 1 & 2, Fontana, 1972.

Munroe, Myles.
Releasing Your Potential, Destiny Image Publishers, 1992.
Understanding Your Potential, Destiny Image Publishers, 1991.

Myers, David.
The Pursuit of Happiness, Aquarian Press, 1993.

Pascal, Blaise.
Pensees, Penguin Books, 1966.

Peck, M. Scott.
The Road Less Travelled, Arrow Books, 1990.
People of the Lie, Arrow, 1988.

Pilzer, Paul Zane.
God Wants You to be Rich, Zane Publishing Inc., 1995.

'Readers Digest'.
Keys to Happiness, Readers Digest, 1957.

Robbins, Anthony.
Awaken the Giant Within, Simon and Schuster, 1991.

Ross, Hugh.
The Creator and the Cosmos, Navpress, 1993.

Schaeffer, Francis.
True Spirituality, Hodder and Stoughton, 1972.

Shames, Laurence.
The Hunger for More, Tins Books, 1989.

Solzhenitsyn, Alexander
East and West, Regal, 1983.

Sproul, R.C.
The Hunger for Significance, Regal, 1983.

Storr, Anthony.
Churchill's Black Dog, Fontana, 1989.

Strobel, Lee.
What Jesus Would Say to... , Zondervan, 1994.

Swenson, Richard.
Margin, Navpress, 1992.

Swindoll, Charles.
Living Above the Level of Mediocrity, Word, 1987.

Thatcher, Margaret.
The Downing Street Years, Harper Collins, 1995.

Treat, Casey.
Reaching Your Destiny, Harrison House, 1987.
Fulfilling Your God-Given Destiny, Thomas Nelson Publishers, 1995.

Whitney, Donald.
Spiritual Disciplines, Navpress, 1991.

Yager, Dexter.
The Mark of a Millionaire, Internet, 1992.

Zacharias, Ravi.
Can a Man Live Without God?, Word Publishing, 1994.
A Shattered Visage, The Real Face of Atheism, Baker Book House, 1990.

Ziglar, Zig.
See You at the Top, Pelican, 1974.